D1559760

Diving & Snorkeling

Puerto Rico

Steve Simonsen

LONELY PLANET PUBLICATIONS
Melbourne • Oakland • London • Paris

Diving & Snorkeling Puerto Rico
- A Lonely Planet Pisces Book

2nd Edition – September, 2000
1st Edition – 1996, Gulf Publishing Company

Published by
Lonely Planet Publications
192 Burwood Road, Hawthorn, Victoria 3122, Australia

Other offices
150 Linden Street, Oakland, California 94607, USA
10a Spring Place, London NW5 3BH, UK
1 rue du Dahomey, 75011 Paris, France

Photographs
by Steve Simonsen unless otherwise noted

Front cover photograph
Heavily encrusted opening at Las Pesones, Desecheo
by Steve Simonsen

Back cover photographs, by Steve Simonsen
Caribbean spiny lobster
Stove-pipe sponge at Canyons, La Parguera
Kayaking at Guánica

The images in this guide are available for licensing
from Lonely Planet Images
email: lpi@lonelyplanet.com.au

ISBN 0 86442 783 2

text & maps © Lonely Planet 2000
photographs © photographers as indicated 2000
dive site maps are Universal Transverse Mercator projection

LONELY PLANET and the Lonely Planet logo are
trademarks of Lonely Planet Publications Pty Ltd.

Printed by H&Y Printing Ltd., Hong Kong

Contents

Author

JESSE SIMONSEN

Steve Simonsen

Since 1978, when he was first certified as an Open Water diver, Steve has been exploring exotic destinations such as French Polynesia, the Red Sea, the Solomon Islands, the Sulu Sea, Micronesia and, closer to home, Mexico, the Bahamas, Puerto Rico, the U.S. and British Virgin Islands and many of the leeward islands in the Caribbean, where he frequently finds himself shooting for various magazines. He is a certified diving instructor for NAUI, PADI and SSI. Steve's colorful Caribbean images have appeared in numerous books, magazines, newspapers and exhibits. Steve, along with his divemaster wife Janet and their son Jesse, runs Marine Scenes, a stock photography agency based year-round on St. John in the U.S. Virgin Islands. Steve teaches photography classes and presents educational slide shows and can be found most days diving and photographing the colorful reefs around St. John.

From the Author

I would like to thank the following people for all their help: Burr Vail (Hacienda Tamarindo, Vieques); Patti and Dennis Johnson and Chipper Leslie (Blue Caribe Dive Center, Vieques); Captain Richard Barone (Vieques Nature Tours); Gene Thomas (former owner of Culebra dive shop); Carmen Cortez and Cathy Casper (El Conquistador Resort & Country Club); David Black (Palomino Divers, Las Croabas); Jim Abbott (Coral Head Divers, Humacao); Nick Benfield (Palmas del Mar Resort, Humacao); Efra Figueroa (Parguera Divers, La Parguera); José Rafols (Aquatic Underwater Adventures, Aguadilla); Efrain (pain) Rodriguez (La Cueva Submarina, Isabela); Beverly Prats (Villa Montaña, Isabela) and all the dive guides who brought me to the wonderful spots described in this book. My thanks to Steve Blount, Bob Morris and James Bartlett of *Caribbean Travel & Life* for sending me on numerous assignments to Puerto Rico which added to the imagery in this book. I would also like to thank Randall Peffer, the author of Lonely Planet's *Puerto Rico*, for his research and information. My greatest thanks have to go to Janet Simonsen, my wife, partner and all-around saint for putting up with me during the writing of the manuscript. Without her help, these words would still be illegible scribble on dozens of legal pads scattered all over the office.

Photography Notes

Steve uses two types of underwater cameras: Nikon 8008s in an Aquatica A80 housing or Nikonos V. The cameras are loaded with Fujichrome Provia 100 and Velvia 50 films. For lighting with either system, he uses dual Ikelite 300 strobes or dual Nikon SB105s. For lenses, Nikkor 16mm, Fisheye 15mm, Rectilinear 20mm, 24mm, 35mm, 55mm Micro or 105mm Micro do the trick. Onland, Steve uses a Nikon F100, an SB26 Speedlight and a Lowepro backpack. Favorite topside lenses include 300mm f2.8 , 80–200mm f2.8, 20 mm, 24mm and 55mm. Steve uses very few filters, but a polarizer comes in handy in the tropics. For commercial photography, he shoots a Mamiya 645 with Speedotron studio lights and scans images using a Nikon Coolscan LS1000.

From the Publisher

This second edition was produced in Lonely Planet's U.S. office under direction from Roslyn Bullas, the Pisces Books publishing manager. Wendy Smith edited the book with invaluable contributions from fellow editor Sarah Hubbard and proofreading from Kevin Anglin. Emily Douglas designed the book and cover. Sara Nelson, Patrick Bock and John Spelman created the maps, which were adapted from the author's extensive base maps, under the supervision of U.S. Cartogrtaphy Manager Alex Guilbert. Portions of this text were adapted from Lonely Planet's *Puerto Rico*.

Pisces Pre-Dive Safety Guidelines

Before embarking on a scuba diving, skin diving or snorkeling trip, carefully consider the following to help ensure a safe and enjoyable experience:

- Possess a current diving certification card from a recognized scuba diving instructional agency (if scuba diving)

- Be sure you are healthy and feel comfortable diving

- Obtain reliable information about physical and environmental conditions at the dive site (e.g., from a reputable local dive operation)

- Be aware of local laws, regulations and etiquette about marine life and environment

- Dive at sites within your experience level; if possible, engage the services of a competent, professionally trained dive instructor or divemaster

Underwater conditions vary significantly from one region, or even site, to another. Seasonal changes can significantly alter site and dive conditions. These differences influence the way divers dress for a dive and what diving techniques they use.

There are special requirements for diving in any area, regardless of location. Before your dive, ask about environmental characteristics that can affect your diving and how trained local divers deal with these considerations.

Warning & Request

Things change—dive site conditions, regulations, topside information. Nothing stays the same for long. Your feedback on this book will be used to help update and improve the next edition. Excerpts from your correspondence may appear in *Planet Talk*, our quarterly newsletter, or *Comet*, our monthly email newsletter. Please let us know if you do not want your letter published or your name acknowledged.

Correspondence can be addressed to:
Lonely Planet Publications
Pisces Books
150 Linden Street
Oakland, CA 94607
email: pisces@lonelyplanet.com

Introduction

The smallest of the Caribbean Sea's Greater Antilles island group, Puerto Rico stands as the gatekeeper between the larger islands to the west and the long arc of the Lesser Antilles to the east. This strategic location, along with the island's status as a U.S. Commonwealth, makes Puerto Rico the commercial and political hub of the Caribbean.

For visitors, Puerto Rico is one of the Caribbean's most enticing destinations, offering all the rich cultural attractions of the Spanish-speaking Caribbean alongside unspoiled natural attractions and the amenities you expect from the region's top vacation destinations. In Old San Juan, the island's dramatic seaside colonial capital, travelers will enjoy dozens of historical buildings and museums, trendy boutiques and galleries, fine restaurants and sizzling nightlife. The El Yunque rainforest, at the island's east end, offers excellent hiking and bird-watching in its lush, verdant confines. Watersports enthusiasts will enjoy the beaches of the west and northwest, including Rincón, the island's surfing mecca. The island's several phosphorescent bays—mangrove bays that boast a high concentration of bioluminescent organisms,

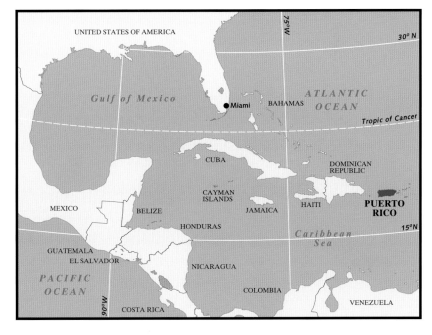

which cast a distinctive and eerie blue light when disturbed by motion—are another major attention grabber.

Divers come to Puerto Rico to experience varied dive regions with vibrant reef life and extraordinarily clear waters. Because the nearshore visibility around the mainland tends to be poor, many of Puerto Rico's best dive sites are around the offshore islands and cays that lie northeast, east and west of the main island. Some of the finest diving and snorkeling sites surround Puerto Rico's four satellite islands—to the east, Culebra and Vieques are reached by small planes and passenger ferries, while to the west, Desecheo and Mona are wildlife refuges usually visited as daytrips. Other impressive diving profiles include the dramatic La Parguera wall several miles off the south shore and the healthy reefs of the Cabo Rojo region, which dive operators have only recently begun to explore.

Though Puerto Rico has a handful of large, high-profile resorts with established dive and watersports services, most of the island's dive industry is characterized by small operations run by charismatic local divemasters. Divers often stay in small, locally run hotels and guest houses.

The 54 dive sites covered in this book represent a range of the best and most popular sites around the Puerto Rican mainland and its smaller satellite islands. The sites are divided into eight distinct diving regions, starting with Vieques and Culebra—the "Spanish Virgin Islands"—and ringing the island's east, south and west coasts before ending with the impressive sites around Isla Desecheo off the west coast. Information about location, depth range, access and expertise level is provided for each site. You'll also find detailed descriptions of each site, noting conditions, underwater topography and the marine life you can expect to see. The Marine Life section provides a gallery of Puerto Rico's common fish and invertebrate life. Though this book is not intended to be a stand-alone travel guide, the Practicalities and Overview sections offer useful information about the islands, while the Activities & Attractions section provides ideas about how to spend your time out of the water.

Overview

Cartographers group Puerto Rico with the Caribbean's three largest islands—Cuba, Jamaica and Hispaniola—to make up the Greater Antilles. However, at just 100 miles (160km) long and 35 miles (56km) wide, Puerto Rico is clearly the little sister of the group. Puerto Rico is 1,000 miles (1,600km) southeast of Miami. Four satellite islands—Desecheo and Mona to the west, Culebra and Vieques to the east—and a host of cays hug the shores of the main island. The perimeter of the island measures just over 300 miles (480km), but the ragged texture of the coast gives Puerto Rico about 750 miles (1,200km) of tidal shoreline.

History

Archaeologists have traced human habitation of Puerto Rico to the 1st century AD, when it was settled by a group known as Los Arcaícos (the Archaics), who are thought to have traveled south from present-day Florida in large rafts hewn from trees. The Igneris (an Arawak group) arrived around AD 300 after expanding up the Lesser Antilles island chain from the Orinoco River basin of present-day Venezuela. They settled coastal Puerto Rico, bringing with them well-developed skills in pottery-making, fishing and canoe-building.

A second wave of Arawaks, the Taínos, reached the island's shores in about AD 600. Archaeological evidence and reports from the first European explorers indicate that the Taínos traveled throughout the West Indies, establishing scattered agricultural settlements as they went. The Taínos eventually centered their civilization in Hispaniola and Puerto Rico, where they evolved a sophisticated culture. The cultural legacy of the Taínos in Puerto Rico remains strong—islanders often refer to Puerto Rico by its Taíno name Borinquen and to themselves as *boricua* (rather than the formal Spanish appellation of *puertorriqueño*).

During the 15th century, the Caribs left the northern shoulder of South America. Master mariners and ruthless warriors, they spread rapidly through the Lesser Antilles. By the fall of 1493, the Caribs were raiding the southeastern coast of Borinquen. Whole Taíno communities took refuge in the island's mountainous interior, and the battle lines between the Taínos and Caribs were drawn along the eastern threshold of the island.

Historians estimate the Taíno population of Borinquen at about 30,000 when Christopher Columbus (Cristobal Colón in Spanish) encountered the island on his second trip to the New World in 1493. These first Europeans found an island scattered with dozens of Taíno communities, each with 300 to 600 inhabitants living within a sharply defined social structure presided over by a *cacique* (chief).

In July 1508, the Spanish established the island's first colony (west of present-day San Juan, a few miles inland from the north coast) with the intent of mining for gold. But the settlement was vulnerable to attack from Indians and malaria-carrying mosquitoes, and the colony was largely evacuated in favor of a small island with a dramatic headland guarding the entrance to a large, protected bay on the north shore of the island. The colonists originally called their new settlement Puerto Rico (meaning Rich Port), but usage eventually applied this name to the whole island. The little fortified town became known as San Juan, after the original Spanish name for the island.

With the search for gold a fading memory, settlers turned to agriculture for profit, cultivating bananas, rice, plantains, ginger, oranges, lemons and sugarcane. Sugarcane flourished and by 1530 a full-scale plantation society was firmly established, with West African slaves making up about half the island's population. Slavery was abolished on the island in 1873, but the African influence on Puerto Rican culture is evident in nearly every cultural realm.

Despite attacks by the French and the British, the Spanish retained control of the island throughout the next several centuries. The colonists battled hurricanes, disease and the uncertainties of a cash-crop economy to become the thriving hub of the Caribbean shipping circuit. By the end of the 19th century, the Spanish had lost nearly all their power in the Americas and the U.S. was perhaps Puerto Rico's principle economic partner. In 1868, a growing independence movement spurred a brief revolution. The Spanish-American War of 1898 resulted in the transfer of Puerto Rico from the Spanish to the U.S.

The island has been under United States sovereignty since 1898. In 1951, Puerto Rico ratified its own constitution, creating the Commonwealth of Puerto Rico. It retains a special relationship with the U.S. whereby islanders are U.S. citizens, but residents do not vote in federal elections and do not have voting representatives in the U.S. Congress.

The second half of the 20th century saw a rise of on-island industry and a cultural free flow between the island and the U.S. mainland, particularly New York City. A substantial political movement for U.S. statehood resulted in plebiscites in 1993 and 1998. The proposal failed by a narrow margin in both cases. These defeats were assisted by a marginal but vocal independence movement. Puerto Rico's status as a U.S. Commonwealth is unlikely to change in the near future.

Geography

Like most of the islands ringing the Caribbean Sea, Puerto Rico owes its existence to a series of volcanic events that took place along the dividing line between the North American and Caribbean tectonic plates. These eruptions built up layers of lava and igneous rock and created an island with four distinct geographical zones: the central mountains, karst country, the coastal plain and the coastal dry forest.

At the heart of the island, running east to west, stands a spine of steep, wooded mountains called the Cordillera Central. The peak of Cerro de Punta rises 4,389ft (1,317m) near the center of the island, marking Puerto Rico's highest point. At the eastern end of the Cordillera Central, the 3,496ft (1,049m) El Yunque gathers a miasma of clouds to its slopes and creates a setting for a dramatic tropical rainforest park which is home to more than 240 tree species.

In the north, the lower slopes of the Cordillera give way to foothills, beaches and a region known as karst country. In this part of the island, erosion has worn away the limestone, leaving a karstic terrain of dramatic sinkholes, hillocks and caves.

The island's northern fringe spreads out into a coastal plain averaging about 10 miles (16km) wide, while the coastal plain on the south side is narrower, only a few miles wide. The dry southwest region around Guánica sustains an unusual desert-like wilderness called a tropical coastal dry forest. These low-lying hills make up the world's largest tract of coastal dry forest and are part of the Guánica Biosphere Reserve. The reserve boasts a rich collection of trees, cacti and migratory birds found nowhere else on the island.

To the northeast, the Puerto Rican mainland is linked to the Virgin Islands by an undersea plateau dotted with many smaller islands and cays. The diving in the northeast near Fajardo and around Vieques and Culebra is characterized by colorful fringing reefs that rarely dip below 80ft (24m).

In the southwest region near Guánica and La Parguera, another broad subsea plateau extends up to 10 miles (16km) away from shore. It averages about 65ft (20m) deep until it takes a giant plunge to a shelf at 600ft (180m) before dropping off again to the extremes of the Venezuelan Basin.

Fifty miles (80km) off Puerto Rico's west coast, in some of the Caribbean's roughest waters, lies the legendary diving paradise of Mona. The west's other, closer offshore diving island is Desecheo, just a stone's throw from the depths of the Atlantic Ocean's Puerto Rican Trench. The trench, which runs roughly parallel to the mainland's north coast, is home to the Milwaukee Depth—at 27,493 (8,380m), this is the deepest point in the Atlantic Ocean and the second-deepest recorded point in the world.

The southwest is mainly tropical coastal dry forest.

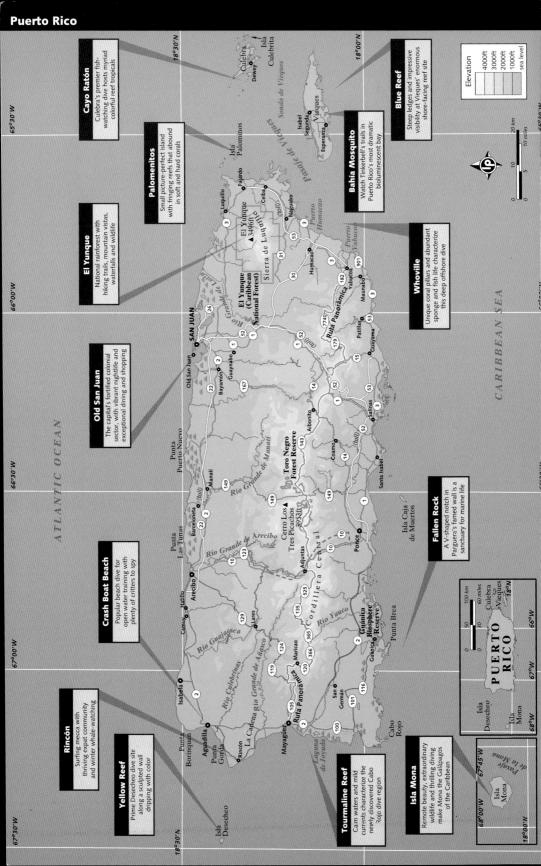

Puerto Rico

Cayo Ratón
Culebra's premier fish-watching dive hosts myriad colorful reef tropicals

Palomenitos
Small picture-perfect island with fringing reefs that abound in soft and hard corals

El Yunque
National rainforest with hiking trails, mountain vistas, waterfalls and wildlife

Blue Reef
Steep ledges and impressive visibility at Vieques' enormous shore-facing reef site

Bahía Mosquito
Watch Tinkerbell's trails in Puerto Rico's most dramatic bioluminescent bay

Old San Juan
The capital's fortified colonial sector, with vibrant nightlife and exceptional dining and shopping

Whoville
Unique coral pillars and abundant sponge and fish life characterize this deep offshore dive

Crash Boat Beach
Popular beach dive for open water training with plenty of critters to spy

Fallen Rock
A V-shaped notch in Parguera's famed wall is a sanctuary for marine life

Rincón
Surfing mecca with thriving expat community and winter whale-watching

Yellow Reef
Prime Desecheo dive site along a sculpted wall dripping with color

Tourmaline Reef
Calm waters and mild currents characterize the newly discovered Cabo Rojo dive region

Isla Mona
Remote beauty, extraordinary wildlife and thrilling diving make Mona the Galápagos of the Caribbean

Elevation
4000ft
3000ft
2000ft
1000ft
sea level

ATLANTIC OCEAN

CARIBBEAN SEA

PUERTO RICO

El Yunque (Caribbean National Forest)

Toro Negro Forest Reserve

Guánica Biosphere Reserve

Cordillera Central

SAN JUAN

Old San Juan

Practicalities

Climate

Puerto Rico's coastal temperatures average about 73°F (23°C) during the coolest months (January and February) and 80°F (27°C) during the hottest months (July, August and September). While high humidity is as much a fact of life here as in most tropical maritime climates, persistent easterly trade winds and local sea breezes provide some relief. The mountainous interior gets much cooler than the beaches—nighttime temperatures sometimes dip below 50°F (9°C).

Winter (December to April) is generally windier and cooler than summer. December through February are usually the driest months of the year. May to November tend to be rainy, usually with heavy daytime tropical cloudbursts that last less than an hour. Hurricane season comes during the hottest and wettest

Killer Storms

The word "hurricane," denoting fierce cyclonic storms with winds in excess of 75mph (120km/h), comes to English and Spanish from the Taíno god of malevolence, Jurakán. Generally, the "seeds" of these storms begin to grow off the west coast of Africa, then migrate across the Atlantic to the Caribbean driven by trade winds. Here they linger and pick up moisture and energy before moving north through the Caribbean and/or the Gulf of Mexico. Eventually, many of these storms pose a threat to the southern and eastern U.S. coasts.

Puerto Rico suffered devastation from three storms—Hugo, Marilyn and Hortense—in the 10 years preceding 1998. Just when islanders were beginning to think that enough was enough, the so-called storm of the century, Georges, struck a direct blow. On September 21, 1998, Georges tore into Puerto Rico with sustained winds of more than 110mph (180km/h), causing damages estimated in excess of US$15 billion before going on to pulverize the Dominican Republic, Haiti, Cuba, the Florida Keys and the U.S. Gulf Coast.

But the island was ready. Fewer than a half-dozen people were killed. Most telephone service was uninterrupted. Shipping and air traffic resumed within 24 hours, and all major roads were cleared of debris. Amazingly, the government restored water and electricity to more than half of the island within five days (the less-powerful Hurricane Hugo had disrupted basic services for more than two weeks in 1989).

Good, long-range storm predictions (broadcast widely on TV and radio and in newspapers), thorough preparation and storm-conscious building practices went a long way toward reducing casualties and property damage. A month after Georges, life for most Puerto Ricans and travelers was back to normal. Unfortunately, Puerto Rico's poorer and less-prepared neighbors—the Dominican Republic, Haiti and Cuba—suffered from a lack of shelters and basic services, while mourning more than 500 lost lives.

months—July to October—with September being the most common month for a hurricane to strike.

Despite the concerns of hurricane season, the best conditions for diving—warm water, calm seas and good visibility—occur in August, September and October. Summer water temperatures range from 80 to 84°F (27 to 29°C), while winter water temperatures are 77 to 80°F (25 to 27°C).

Language

Puerto Rico is an officially bilingual country and most educated islanders are fluent in both English and Spanish. That said, Spanish is always the language in which island-born Puerto Ricans speak to one another as a matter of cultural pride. Many older citizens and Puerto Ricans living outside areas frequented by English-speaking travelers and businesspeople speak only Spanish.

One of the many unique elements of Boricua—the language of Borinquen (the island's Taíno name, still used widely by locals)—is the linguistic mixing that stems from the influence of English. Even in the more remote parts of the island, elements of American English filter in from Puerto Rican barrios on the mainland and from TV, radio, film and advertising. Puerto Ricans have appropriated some English words and idioms outright, but more often the roots of English words have been turned into Spanish-sounding verbs and nouns.

Locals enjoy a lively game of dominoes under the shade of a large tree in Old San Juan.

Getting There

San Juan's Aeropuerto Internacional Luis Muñoz Marín (LMM) lies just 2 miles (3km) east of the city in the beachfront suburb of Isla Verde. Half of all flights to and from the Caribbean pass through this world-class facility, so it has all the imaginable amenities—dining, shopping and currency-exchange facilities rival those of other U.S. ports of entry.

San Juan is the Caribbean hub for American Airlines, which has the largest number of daily flights in and out of the region and offers easy access to and from U.S. cities. San Juan is also served by other North American carriers via Miami and a score of other mainland U.S. cities. British Airways has services from London, Iberia flies from Madrid and Lufthansa's subsidiary Condor provides travelers with a link from Frankfurt.

Most visitors arrive and depart from San Juan, but two other airports on the island offer occasional service to and from the U.S.—Ponce's Aeropuerto de Mercedita on the south coast, and the bomber strip at Aguadilla's Aeropuerto Rafael Hernández, on the island's northwest tip. San Juan's original airport at Isla Grande, on the Bahía de San Juan in the Miramar district, services private aircraft and the bulk of commuter flights to the Spanish Virgin Islands.

Gateway City - San Juan

The 300 sq miles (480 sq km) of metropolitan San Juan are home to more than a third of the island's population, a concentration that speaks to the attractions of the capital. The phalanx of high-rise condominiums standing guard over the shores of Isla Verde, Condado and Miramar is a powerful symbol of San Juan's

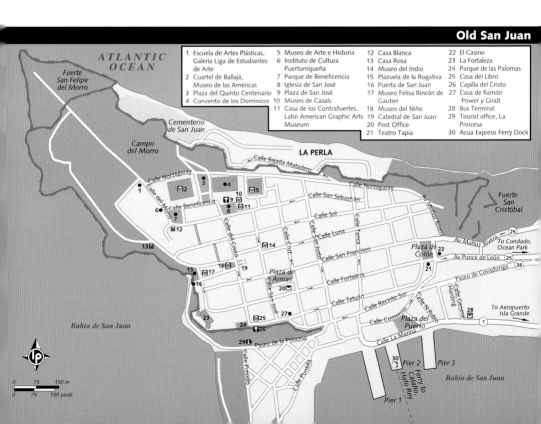

Old San Juan

1	Escuela de Artes Plásticas, Galería Liga de Estudiantes de Arte	5	Museo de Arte e Historia
2	Cuartel de Ballajá, Museo de las Américas	6	Instituto de Cultura Puertorriqueña
3	Plaza del Quinto Centenario	7	Parque de Beneficencia
4	Convento de los Dominicos	8	Iglesia de San José
		9	Plaza de San José
		10	Museo de Casals
		11	Casa de los Contrafuertes, Latin American Graphic Arts Museum

12 Casa Blanca
13 Casa Rosa
14 Museo del Indio
15 Plazuela de la Rogativa
16 Puerta de San Juan
17 Museo Felisa Rincón de Gautier
18 Museo del Niño
19 Catedral de San Juan
20 Post Office
21 Teatro Tapia

22 El Casino
23 La Fortaleza
24 Parque de las Palomas
25 Casa del Libro
26 Capilla del Cristo
27 Casa de Ramón Power y Giralt
28 Bus Terminal
29 Tourist office, La Princesa
30 Acua Expreso Ferry Dock

prosperity, as are the spit-and-polish care that owners lavish on their guest houses in Ocean Park, the grandeur of posh hotels and world-class restaurants, and the crowds of chic patrons in its casinos and clubs.

Of course, the undisputed crown jewel of the metropolis is the magnificent walled city that the world has come to know as Old San Juan. Old San Juan is a working, breathing community rife with cobblestone streets, pastel-colored town houses, Romanesque arches, wrought-iron balconies, intimate courtyards and striking vistas. By day it functions as the seat of both the city and Commonwealth governments. By night the old town becomes a pulsing center of nightlife. Beyond the walls of Old San Juan, the modern city has its hidden joys as well; look for them in the neighborhoods where university students reside, artists paint and the songs of the next generation of salsa legends fill the streets.

Getting Around

Perhaps because Puerto Rico is relatively small, or perhaps because it has a strong

"car culture," the Commonwealth's domestic air transportation system is rather basic. If you are in a hurry, or do not want to deal with a rental car, you can catch daily flights between San Juan, Ponce and Mayagüez. However, the bulk of Puerto Rico's domestic flights link San Juan to the Spanish Virgin Islands of Culebra and Vieques.

Públicos—the shared taxis that take passengers along a set route—form the backbone of Puerto Rico's public transportation system and represent the principal way that locals travel between island towns. These vehicles tend to be minivans filled with bench seats and can be identified by the letters

A scenic highway leads through the El Yunque rainforest.

P or PD on the license plate. The van's destination is usually posted on top of the windshield. Fares are inexpensive and fluctuate depending on the number of people in the van.

Driving is the most convenient way to get around the countryside, see small towns, cross sprawling suburbs and explore wide-open spaces. Visitors venturing outside San Juan and other large cities will find renting a car to be an attractive option. Puerto Rico has the best roads in the Caribbean and probably in all of Latin America. If you do drive in Puerto Rico, use extreme caution and drive defensively, as Puerto Rican drivers are often quite aggressive. A good road map—available at bookstores and newsstands all over the island—is also essential.

All major U.S. car rental agencies are represented in Puerto Rico. Most rental companies require that you have a major credit card, that you be at least 25 years old and that you have a valid driver's license. A U.S. driver's license is valid in Puerto Rico for three months.

Vieques & Culebra

Flights leave for Vieques and Culebra regularly from San Juan (20-minute flight) and from Fajardo (15-minute flight). Isla Nena Air Service (☎ 888-263-6213) departs from LMM, and Vieques Air Link (☎ 888-901-9247) leaves from Isla Grande; both airlines also depart from Fajardo.

Modern high-speed ferries depart from Fajardo for Vieques and Culebra several times a day. The trip to either island is inexpensive and takes about an hour. For information and reservations (recommended on weekends), call the Puerto Rican Port Authority (☎ 800-981-2005 or ☎ 741-4761 on Vieques or ☎ 742-3161 on Culebra). Note: If you're headed to the islands, don't bother to rent a car until you get there.

Entry

As a U.S. Commonwealth, Puerto Rico subscribes to all the laws that apply to traveling and border crossing in the U.S. Foreign visitors to the island (other than Canadians) must bring their passports. Canadians must have proper proof of Canadian citizenship, such as a citizenship card with photo ID or a passport. All travelers should bring a driver's license and any health-insurance or travel-insurance cards.

Visitors from other countries must have a valid passport, and many visitors are also required to have a U.S. visa, which is generally good for one or five years and valid for multiple entries. Under the Visa Waiver Pilot Program, citizens of certain countries (including Australia, New Zealand and the U.K.) can visit the U.S. for tourism or business purposes for up to 90 days without a visa. Check the U.S. State Department's website (travel.state.gov/visa_services.html) for detailed current information about visa requirements and application processes.

Time

Puerto Rico is on Atlantic Standard Time, one hour ahead of Eastern Standard Time and four hours behind GMT. When it's noon in Puerto Rico, it's 11am in New York, 4pm in London, 8am in San Francisco and 1am the following morning in Sydney. Daylight saving time is not observed.

Money

The U.S. dollar is the official currency of Puerto Rico. All major credit cards are widely accepted. The government tax on room charges is 7% (9% at hotels and casinos). Some hotels automatically add a 10 to 15% service charge to your bill. A 15 to 20% tip is expected in restaurants. There is no departure tax.

Electricity

As in the U.S., voltage in Puerto Rico is 110 volts/60 cycles and plugs have two flat pins or three (two flat, one round) pins. Plugs with three pins don't fit into a two-hole socket, but adapters are easy to find at hardware stores.

Weights & Measures

Puerto Rico is a bit confusing around these issues. Like the rest of Latin America, islanders use the metric system to measure the volume of gasoline and highway distances. The U.S. influence shows up in the posting of highway speed limits in miles per hour, but distance is posted on the highways in kilometers. Otherwise, temperature is generally measured in degrees Fahrenheit, length in feet and yards, and weight in pounds and ounces.

This book provides both imperial and metric measurements, except for specific references within dive site descriptions, which are given in imperial units only. For reference, use the conversion chart inside the back cover of this book.

What to Bring

As a U.S. Commonwealth and the economic center of the Caribbean, Puerto Rico has just about anything you'd want in the form of clothing, gear, supplies, medicines and favorite foods readily available. For clothing, light cotton garments and a couple of bathing suits will meet almost all of your needs. Though you won't need formal wear, you might want to bring something a little fancier for nights out in Old San Juan and the casinos. Comfortable walking shoes are essential for exploring the cobblestone streets of Old San Juan and the trails of the forest reserves. Bring a sweater or fleece pullover for cool or windy nights on the coast or in the mountains. A light rain jacket or umbrella can come in handy, and a flashlight is useful for dark nights.

As for diving equipment, it is always recommended to bring your own mask, fins, snorkel, BC and regulator, though all of these are also readily available for rental. Dive computers are extremely useful, but unfortunately are not always available to rent. In summer (May to October), a dive skin, shorty or 3mm wetsuit will be sufficient for most people. In winter (November to April), you'll want at least a one- or two-piece 3mm suit; a 5mm or even 6mm wetsuit will keep you comfortable on long dives near cold currents or on rainy days.

Underwater Photography

It is best to bring or rent all photo and video equipment and film from home. Slide film and E-6 processing is available from specialty photo shops in San Juan, Mayagüez and Ponce, but is scarce otherwise. If you are serious about underwater photography on your trip, be sure to bring backup cameras, strobes and sync cords. One trick is to assemble all your equipment at home, then disassemble everything and pack it on the spot so nothing is left behind. Underwater photo and video classes are not widely taught in Puerto Rico.

Business Hours

Business hours are generally 8am to 5pm, but there are certainly no hard-and-fast rules. Shops are usually open weekdays and Saturday from 9 or 10am to 5 or 6pm and Sunday from 11am to 5pm. Some shops stay open until 9pm on Friday evening, and shops in malls tend to stay open later in general. Post offices are open weekdays 8am to 4 or 5:30pm, and some are open Saturday 8am to 1pm. Banking hours are usually weekdays 8am to 2:30pm and Saturday 9:45am to noon.

The reef's vivid colors are enhanced with handheld lights.

Accommodations

Lodging rates in Puerto Rico vary significantly (sometimes more than 30%) from season to season and even from day to day, as hotels adjust rates according to the perceived demand. In general, rates are highest from December 15 to the end of May. They remain high during June, July and August, when many island families take their vacations. Rates are lowest from September to December 14. Puerto Rico offers a wide range of "luxury" or "deluxe" establishments as well as self-contained resorts with golf courses, restaurants, spas and tennis courts.

Puerto Rico's small hotels and guest houses offer alternatives to the high prices and insularity that can come with resort hotels in the tourist zones. Guest houses differ vastly from one to another—the cheapest establishments may have certain inconveniences such as a shared bath, while more upscale options might be in a quaint country home or urban beach house. Short and extended home or

Paradores

The Puerto Rican government operates a network of 18 *paradores* (inns) fashioned after a similar network in Spain. These inns are found throughout the Commonwealth near areas of historical, natural or cultural interest. There are inns near San Germán, Puerto Rico's second oldest city, and on the grounds of an old coffee plantation, high in the mountains. Other paradores provide access to natural areas like the karst limestone region, which is loaded with caves and thermal springs, the

panoramic cliffs along the north shore and the El Yunque rainforest. Divers and snorkelers will take particular interest in inns near the world-famous west coast surfing beaches, seaside communities along the south coast including La Parguera, and the popular watersports areas on east coast.

The paradores differ from one to another not only in setting but also in atmosphere, with facilities ranging from guest houses in rural surroundings to hotels near golf courses and airports. All of the paradores share the same good service and family atmosphere.

In addition to the paradores, the Commonwealth of Puerto Rico maintains a cluster of rental cottages (called vacation centers) around the island in Arroyo, Boquerón, Anasco, Humacao and Maricao. These rentals are available to family groups only. For more information on either the paradores or the rental cottages contact the Puerto Rican Tourism Company (see Tourist Offices in the Listings section).

Hacienda Juanita, a parador on an historic coffee plantation near Maricao.

villa rentals are very popular in Puerto Rico as well. These can be a particularly good value if you are willing to stay in one place for a week or more.

Camping is the cheapest accommodation and can be an enjoyable approach to a vacation, though divers with gear may find it inconvenient. Visitors with a car and a tent can take advantage of dozens of private and public campgrounds around the island.

Puerto Rico boasts a handful of resorts with dive operators on the premises, but most hotels will simply recommend a dive operator nearby. There are few, if any, dive packages.

Dining & Food

Puerto Rico's cuisine reflects the Commonwealth's fusion of Taíno, Spanish and African heritage. Some of the most traditional dishes are soups and stews that use unique island vegetables—such as *yautia* (tanier), *batata* (sweet potato), *yuca* (cassava), *chayote* (squash), *berzas* (collard greens) and *grelos* (turnip greens)—to add texture, taste and vitamins. Perhaps the most popular island stew is *asopao de pollo*, a rich and spicy chicken stew that is fragrant with the distinctive seasoning called *adobo*. Puerto Rican cuisine is not spicy-hot, but exceptionally tasty. Ingredients such as seafood, meats, poultry, starchy vegetables and delectable spices, including the popular *sofrito* mix, are combined in one-of-a-kind recipes. Puerto Rico is justly famous worldwide for its high-quality rums and rich local coffees.

The Puerto Rico Tourism Company sponsors a program called Mesones Gastronómicos, which has identified a collection of recommended restaurants around the island that feature Puerto Rican cuisine and maintain high standards. A list of these restaurants can be found in the bimonthly tourist magazine *Qué Pasa*.

Shopping

Shoppers will find a lot of tempting, pretty things in the shops of Old San Juan, Condado and Ponce, but few bargains. Since Puerto Rico is not a duty-free port, the only economic advantage to shopping in Puerto Rico is that there is no sales tax.

Travelers looking for souvenirs are drawn to the island's folk arts. *Santos* are probably the most popular purchase, but these carved religious figures can cost well over US$100. *Mundillo*, the intricately woven island-made lace, is also a popular purchase, as are woven hammocks. You can also pick up *vejigantes*, masks typical of those worn in the fiestas at Ponce and Loíza. Island-made macramé and ceramic items are also widely available in shops catering to tourists. Inexpensive purchases include local rums and coffees. Old San Juan offers a great variety of art galleries, jewelry shops, quality leather-goods stores and apparel outlets. The Condado sector is famous for its exclusive boutiques and fashion designer shops. Plaza las Américas, in the heart of the San Juan metropolitan area, is the largest shopping mall in the Caribbean with nearly 200 stores.

Activities & Attractions

Puerto Rico has enough topside attractions to please every type of visitor. San Juan offers some of the best in Caribbean cultural attractions, from museums, historic buildings and city walks, to contemporary art galleries, lively restaurants and bars and hot salsa shows. The rest of the island offers plenty of natural attractions. Surfing and watersports beaches ring the Puerto Rican mainland and offshore islands, while the rugged interior is home to a rainforest, mountain peaks, caves and a network of scenic rural highways.

Old San Juan

As recently as three decades ago, the fortified colonial sector of Puerto Rico's capital was a decaying red-light district with more than 400 abandoned buildings. Impressively restored, today's Old San Juan treats strollers to the charms of a dramatic natural setting, historic architecture, fine cultural institutions and a spirited community. Here, 500 years of Spanish colonial history blend almost seamlessly

Old San Juan's cobbled streets bring you by the ramparts of the walled colonial city.

with contemporary Caribbean culture as you walk along lamplit cobblestone streets. Colorful town houses rich with iron balconies and potted plants line your way. Historic forts, churches and museums—many with free admission—open their doors to you for exploration.

Ideally, a traveler will spend days, weeks or even months soaking up the tropical flavor of Old San Juan and yielding to the town's mood swings, from pensive mornings to passionate nights. Still, Old San Juan is so compact that even visitors with little time can get a feel for this World Heritage site. In fact, you can complete a tour of the old city's main sites during a three-hour walk. Major sites include the San Felipe del Morro fort; the El Convento hotel, housed in a 17th-century convent building; La Fortaleza Street, lined with shops and pubs; pigeon-filled Parque de las Palomas; and Paseo de la Princesa, a quaint 19th-century esplanade.

Parque de las Cavernas del Río Camuy

The Camuy River Cave Park is home to one of the largest cave systems in the world, as well as the world's third-longest underground river. Your visit begins with a film about the caves at the visitors center. Then you take a trolley bus down a spiraling road through the jungle into a 200ft- (60m-) deep sinkhole. From there, you take a 45-minute guided walk through the cave past enormous stalagmites and stalactites and into rooms littered with boulders. At one point, the ceiling of the cavern reaches a height of 170ft (50m); at another, you see the Río Camuy rushing through a tunnel. After leaving the cave from a side passage, you take another tram to the Tres Pueblos sinkhole, which measures 650ft (20m) across and drops 400ft (120m). Other attractions include 42 petroglyphs found in Cueva Catedral (Cathedral Cave) and the Mina del Río Camuy, a touristy invention where you can sluice for semiprecious stones.

The caves are open 8am to 4pm Wednesday to Sunday. The last tour leaves at 2pm if you want to see all three areas, or at 3:45pm if you want to see just one sinkhole. The park is at Km 18.9 on Highway 129, a few miles north of Lares. Since the cave park is on the road to Arecibo, your visit can be combined with a trip to the nearby Arecibo observatory.

Observatorio de Arecibo

The opening scenes of the Jodie Foster movie *Contact* were filmed at the Arecibo observatory, which is home the world's largest radio telescope. The 20-acre (8-hectare) dish is set into a natural sinkhole the size of 22 football fields. The observatory, which is used to study planets, stars and distant galaxies, is operated by Cornell University astronomers and is part of the SETI (Search for Extraterrestrial Intelligence) program. The observatory is open for self-guided tours noon to 4pm Wednesday to Friday and 9am to 4pm weekends and holidays. There is also an educational exhibit and fun science store for children.

El Yunque

The 28,000-acre (11,200-hectare) Caribbean National Rainforest is known as El Yunque (pronounced El JOON-kay), after its distinctive 3,496ft (1,049m) central peak. Taíno Indians believed that protective gods lived in the high peaks of the Luquillo mountains. Though *yunque* means anvil in Spanish, the name is actually a bastardization of Yukiyá, an important Taíno spirit.

The preserve holds the distinction of being the only tropical rainforest in the U.S. National Forest Service. More than 240 species of trees and 1,000 plant species thrive here. The El Portal Tropical Forest Center, which offers maps and interactive exhibits, is a great way to begin your journey. La Coca Falls can be found right along the roadside. An easy hike down a well-maintained trail brings you to La Mina Falls, where you can swim or just cool off in the mist of a pounding waterfall.

Weekends are busy as cars wind along Route 191 through lush tropical vegetation and immense greenery. The park is open 9am to 5pm daily. Arrive early any morning just as the gates are opening and you'll have the place to yourself for nearly two hours. The vegetation, mountain views and hiking trails combine with the sounds of coquí tree frogs and distant thunder to become a truly mystical experience.

Ruta Panorámica

There is no better way to escape the island's tropical heat, crowds and sprawl than to head out on this scenic drive along a chain of roads that follow the island's spine. Along the east-west route you can see the deep volcanic rift called Cañón de San Cristóbal, the mountain town of Barranquitas and the tallest peaks on the island. This is one of the Caribbean's most spectacular drives. A chain of 40 mountain roads stretches 165 miles (266km); it would be difficult or impossible to cover the route in a single day. Instead, several days of short trips would be a good way to experience the verdant Puerto Rican interior. Much of the route is marked with road signs along the way. *Qué Pasa*, the tourist board's bimonthly magazine, offers a map of the route, and most road maps available from island bookstores and newsstands have the route clearly marked.

Whale-Watching

Each winter, groups of humpback whales pass through the Mona Passage between Puerto Rico and the Dominican Republic as part of their annual migration. Observation towers are set up along the roads in Rincón and Aguadilla, and dedicated whale-watching trips set out several times a week during the season from Puerto Real on the west coast. Chances are good that you'll see or hear whales on any dive trip to Isla Desecheo. The season goes from January to March with early arrivals in December and stragglers possible in April.

The scenic Ruta Panorámica is the best way to explore Puerto Rico's mountainous interior.

The whales that pass through these waters are the same as those seen by throngs of whale-watchers off the New England coast, where they spend each summer feeding on krill. Whales breed in precise relation to the amount of food in the water. If food is plentiful up in the North Atlantic, most of the whales return to these warmer tropical waters to breed. Courtship depends upon the male's ability to outperform his rivals with intriguing songs and wild body movements, including spy-hopping, lob-tailing, tail-slapping and breaching. In mating, the whale pair embraces belly to belly and, stroking each other with their pectoral fins, accelerates toward the surface in unison. The two break the surface together and fall away from each other in a tremendous splash.

The gestation period is just under a year and the female returns to the same waters the following year to give birth. Sometime after the newborn calf is lifted to the surface for its first breath, the mother will begin feeding her young the equivalent of 800 glasses of milk each day. The mother and the calf stay around warm water long enough to get the newborn strong and capable of the long journey ahead. The mother eats next to nothing for months until the pair enters into the nutrient-rich waters of the North Atlantic.

Surfing

Ever since the world surfing championships were held at Rincón in 1968, surfers worldwide have recognized the potential of Puerto Rico's surfing scene. Winter months (November through April) are best, as cold fronts create surf all along the north and west coasts.

Well-known sites along Highway 167 near San Juan include Pine Grove, Los Aviones, La Concha and Piñones. Farther east, look for La Pared (near Luquillo) and Racetracks (near Punta Gorda). Inches is a well-known spot along Highway 3 in the southeast near Maunabo.

The island's best surfing, however, is along the northwest coast from Rincón to Isabela. Breaks like Tres Palmas, Marías Beach, Domes, Table Rock, Gas Chambers, Wilderness, Shacks and Jobos Beach attract surfers of tremendous ability. Along the north coast west of San Juan, look for the Hallows, Los Tubos and Kikitas.

Bioluminescent Bays

Puerto Rico boasts at least three bioluminescent bays—Laguna Grande (north of Fajardo), Vieques' Bahía Mosquito (also called Bio Bay) and La Parguera's Bahía Fosforente. In these lagoons, naturally occurring masses of microorganisms provide an eerie nighttime light show, giving off a sudden blue-green phosphorescent sparkle when disturbed by friction or movement.

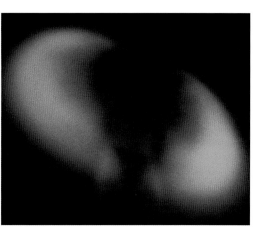

Departing just after dusk, operators in Fajardo, Vieques and La Parguera offer nightly trips to see the sparkling Tinkerbell's trails created by fish fleeing in the wake of an oncoming boat. For the experience of a lifetime, you can swim at night from the boat—with each stroke, the water magically lights up around you. The bioluminescence is a must-see when visiting Puerto Rico and is best observed on cloudy or moonless nights.

A swimmer's moving arms trigger a bioluminescent glow.

Bright Lights, Black Water

The bioluminescence you see in a few of Puerto Rico's sheltered mangrove bays is produced by ocean-born microorganisms known as dinoflagellates. There are a number of dinoflagellate species in tropical waters, but the most abundant in Puerto Rico's phosphorescent bays is *Pirodinium bahamense*. ("Pirodinium" comes from the Latin roots *pyro*, meaning fire, and *dinium*, meaning rotate.)

When movement—from fish, boats or human swimmers, for example—disturbs these creatures, a chemical reaction takes place in their microscopic bodies that creates a flash. Scientists speculate about the purpose of the flash; many think that the dinoflagellates have developed this ability to give off a sudden green light as a defense mechanism to ward off predators.

You can see these microorganisms flashing in Atlantic waters as far north as New England in the summer, but never in the brilliant concentrations appearing in Puerto Rico. As it turns out, enclosed mangrove bays, where narrow canals limit the exchange of water with the open sea, are excellent places for dinoflagellates to breed and live. In a sense, the bay acts as a big trap, and vitamins produced along the shore provide food that fosters reproduction in the corralled microorganisms.

Diving Health & Safety

General Health

Puerto Rico is a generally healthy destination and poses few serious health risks to most visitors. The Commonwealth is free of most tropical diseases such as malaria, yellow fever and cholera.

One concern is dengue fever, a mosquito-borne disease that produces sudden high fever, muscle and joint pain and a rash, which generally subside after a few days. Though the disease itself is untreatable, hospitals can treat the symptoms if necessary. The best way to deal with dengue is to avoid it by using mosquito repellents liberally.

The sun is perhaps the most common concern—any activity in the tropical sun can lead to sunburn, and the heat plus nightly consumption of alcoholic beverages can cause dehydration. Divers should cover up or wear sunscreen and drink plenty of water.

The U.S. Centers for Disease Control & Prevention regularly posts updates on health-related concerns around the world specifically for travelers. Contact the CDC by fax or visit their website. Call (toll-free from the U.S.) ☎ 888-232-3299 and request Document 000005 to receive a list of documents available by fax. The website is www.cdc.gov.

Pre-Trip Preparation

Your general state of health, diving skill level and specific equipment needs are the three most important factors that impact any dive trip. If you honestly assess these before you leave, you'll be well on your way to assuring a safe dive trip.

Diving & Flying

Most divers in Puerto Rico arrive by plane. While it's fine to dive soon *after* flying, it's important to remember that your last dive should be completed at least 12 hours (some experts advise 24 hours, particularly after repetitive dives) *before* your flight to minimize the risk of decompression sickness, caused by residual nitrogen in the blood.

First, if you're not in shape, start exercising. Second, if you haven't dived for a while (six months is too long) and your skills are rusty, do a local dive with an experienced buddy or take a scuba review course. Finally, inspect your dive gear. Feeling good physically, diving with experience and with reliable equipment will not only increase your safety, but will also enhance your enjoyment underwater.

At least a month before your trip, inspect your dive gear. Remember, your regulator should be serviced annually, whether you've used it or not. If you use a dive computer and can replace the battery yourself, change it before the trip or buy a spare one to take along. Otherwise, send the computer to the manufacturer for a battery replacement.

If possible, find out if the dive center rents or services the type of gear you own. If not, you might want to take spare parts or even spare gear. A spare mask is always a good idea.

Purchase any additional equipment you might need, such as a dive light and tank marker light for night diving, a line reel for wreck diving, etc. Make sure you have at least a whistle attached to your BC. Better yet, add a marker tube (also known as a safety sausage or come-to-me).

About a week before taking off, do a final check of your gear, grease o-rings, check batteries and assemble a save-a-dive kit. This kit should at minimum contain extra mask and fin straps, snorkel keeper, mouthpiece, valve cap, zip ties and o-rings. Don't forget to pack a first-aid kit and medications such as decongestants, ear drops, antihistamines and seasickness tablets.

Tips for Evaluating a Dive Operator

First impressions mean a lot. Does the business appear organized and professionally staffed? Does it prominently display a dive affiliation such as NAUI, PADI, SSI, BSAC, CMAS or ACUC? These are both good indications that it adheres to high standards.

When you come to dive, a well-run business will always have paperwork for you to fill out. At the least, someone should look at your certification card and ask when you last dived. If they want to see your logbook or check basic skills in the water, even better.

Rental equipment should be well rinsed. If you see sand or salt crystals, watch out, as their presence could indicate sloppy equipment care. Before starting on your dive, inspect the equipment thoroughly: Check hoses for wear, see that mouthpieces are secure and make sure they've given you a depth gauge and air pressure gauge.

After you gear up and turn on your air, listen for air leaks. Now test your BC: Push the power inflator to make sure it functions correctly and doesn't free-flow; if it fails, get another BC—don't try to inflate it manually; make sure the BC holds air. Then purge your regulator a bit and smell the air. It should be odorless. If you detect an oily or otherwise bad smell, try a different tank, then start searching for another operator.

Medical & Recompression Facilities

Puerto Rico's medical facilities are extensive and modern, but are expensive by European standards. **Ashford Memorial Community Hospital** (☎ 721-2160), in San Juan's Condado area, is probably the best-equipped and most convenient hospital for travelers in the capital. In an **emergency**, call ☎ 911.

With two fully staffed recompression chambers, Puerto Rico is equipped to handle any diving emergency.

U.S. Naval Station Roosevelt Roads
hyperbaric chamber: ☎ 865-4584 or ☎ 865-3636
emergency room: ☎ 865-5997, ☎ 865-5816 or ☎ 865-5818

Administración de Servicios Médicos de Puerto Rico
emergency room: ☎ 777-3535, ☎ 754-3860 or ☎ 754-3549

DAN

Divers Alert Network (DAN) is an international membership association of individuals and organizations sharing a common interest in diving and safety. It operates a 24-hour diving emergency hotline in the U.S.: ☎ **919-684-8111** or

Listen carefully to your divemaster's safety tips.

919-684-4DAN (-4326). The latter accepts collect calls in a dive emergency. Though DAN does not directly provide medical care, it does provide advice on early treatment, evacuation and hyperbaric treatment of diving-related injuries. Divers should contact DAN for assistance as soon as a diving emergency is suspected.

DAN membership is reasonably priced and includes DAN TravelAssist, a membership benefit that covers medical air evacuation from anywhere in the world for any illness or injury. For a small additional fee, divers can get secondary insurance coverage for decompression illness. For membership questions, contact DAN at ☎ 800-446-2671 in the U.S. or ☎ 919-684-2948 elsewhere. DAN can also be reached at www. diversalertnetwork.org.

Diving in Puerto Rico

For many years, divers overlooked Puerto Rico in favor of better-known diving islands in the Caribbean. In recent years, however, well-equipped and professionally run dive operators began to share their pioneering attitude with savvy divers from around the globe. Today, Puerto Rico is building its reputation as an excellent place for cave and cavern diving, adventure-diving trips to remote satellite islands, and sun-drenched shallow coral reefs.

The visibility in the waters around Puerto Rico averages 60 to 75ft (18 to 23m). Near shore and under certain conditions, visibility can drop to about 30ft (9m), while the water offshore is often beautifully clear, with visibility of 100ft (30m) or better. As a result, many of Puerto Rico's best dive sites are several miles offshore. These offshore sites can be exposed to strong currents and heavy surge, and rough weather sometimes prohibits diving at certain sites. Though dive operators are accustomed to making long boat trips to reach the prime sites, rough surface

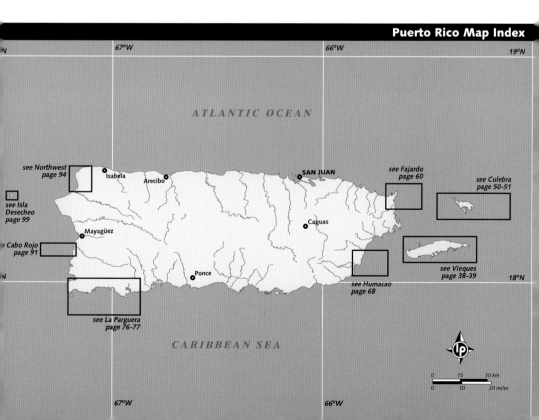

Puerto Rico Map Index

67°W
66°W
19°N

ATLANTIC OCEAN

Isabela
Arecibo
SAN JUAN
Caguas
Mayagüez
Ponce

18°N

CARIBBEAN SEA

67°W
66°W

0   15   30 km
0   10   20 miles

conditions may pose a problem for divers prone to seasickness—consider taking antinausea medication before you set out.

To the northeast, Puerto Rico is linked with the Virgin Islands by an undersea plateau. The diving in this area is done around the many smaller islands and cays—especially around the tranquil islands of Vieques and Culebra, the "Spanish Virgin Islands." These dives feature colorful fringing reefs, which rarely dip below 80ft (24m). Vieques and Culebra are far enough from the Puerto Rican mainland that they require an overnight stay.

Though there are a few convenient dive sites near San Juan, serious divers staying on the north coast head west to the beach dives near Isabela and Agua-dilla, or east to the Fajardo area. Because the waters close to shore around Fajardo have poor visibility, dive operators head out to the clearer waters around the nearby cays and islands.

In the southeast, near Humacao, the continental size of things begins to shape up with deeper diving also a fair distance from shore and excellent visibility, usually 80 to 100ft (24 to 30m). The southwest coast near Guánica and La Parguera offers the most spectacular wall diving on the island. In this area, a long, flat shelf at 65ft (20m) stretches away from the coast to a breathtaking drop. While some of the dive sites are along the shelf, many take you to deep sites along the wall's edge.

Although there are some nearshore dive sites along the placid west coast, adventurous divers arrange boat trips to the legendary Desecheo and Mona islands. Rough conditions often preclude visits to either island (this is especially common for the more remote Mona), but divers who manage to make the trip encounter impressive colorful reefs and pelagic life.

Dive operators in Puerto Rico tend to be more informal than at many Caribbean dive destinations—many shops keep irregular hours, sometimes diving

Underwater San Juan

Though the north coast is not considered Puerto Rico's most notable diving region, divers staying in or near San Juan can take advantage of a number of convenient novice diving and snorkeling spots in the area.

For snorkeling, most visitors prefer **Dog Rock**, the jetty at the public beach near the Condado Plaza Hotel in the Condado area. This site is shallow—not more than 10ft (3m) deep—and offers a good chance to see common Caribbean fish and invertebrates. Another popular snorkel spot is the jetty between the Holiday Inn and the El San Juan on Isla Verde.

For some of the best critter diving in Puerto Rico, go to **Figure 8 Reef** and **Horseshoe Reef** behind the Raddison Normandy Beach Hotel, east of Old San Juan in Puerta Tierra. These shallow sites don't go below 30ft (9m) and beach dives are the norm. Visibility is never excellent in these waters, but the reefs are bursting with fish and invererbate life, including plenty of uncommon and unusual species. Keep an eye out for flying gurnards, batfish, frogfish, searobins and tiny seahorses.

Excellent snorkeling spots line Vieques' north shore, which is also the southern boundary of the infamous Bermuda Triangle

only on weekends. Dive boats usually carry small groups, and in many cases you'll dive with the owner of the shop. Don't be surprised if you have to wait until you're in-country to arrange your dive trips. That said, the Puerto Rico dive industry is growing and new dive sites—particularly in the southwest area around Cabo Rojo—are constantly being discovered.

Snorkeling

Since visibility near the mainland's shores tends to be compromised, the best snorkeling in Puerto Rico takes place around the offshore islands of Vieques and Culebra and around the cays off the Fajardo coast, notably around Palominos. These areas are characterized by abundant fish and invertebrate life. Other snorkel sites include several northwest beaches and a handful of convenient jetties in the San Juan area.

Certification

Puerto Rico is a good place to learn to dive for the first time. Most of Puerto Rico's dive operators offer Open Water certification courses for individuals or groups.

Many can also do check-out dives if you have done your coursework at home. It is best to arrange these courses before your trip to ensure that there will be no conflict between certifying agencies. Another option is to take a Discover Scuba course (sometimes called a Resort course), which provides a chance to try a dive without actually becoming a certified diver.

Dive Site Icons

The symbols at the beginning of each dive site description provide a quick summary of some of the important characteristics of each site:

 Good snorkeling or free-diving site.

 Remains or partial remains of a wreck can be seen at this site.

 Sheer wall or drop-off.

 Deep dive. Features of this dive are found in water deeper than 90ft (27m).

 Strong currents may be encountered at this site.

 Strong surge (the horizontal movement of water caused by waves) may be encountered at this site.

 Drift dive. Because of strong currents and/or difficulty in anchoring, a drift dive is recommended at this site.

 Shore dive. This site can be accessed from shore.

 Poor visibility. The site often has visibility of less than 25ft (8m).

 Caves or caverns are prominent features of this site. Only experienced cave divers should explore inner cave areas.

Pisces Rating System for Dives & Divers

The dive sites in this book are rated according to the following diver skill-level rating system. These are not absolute ratings but apply to divers at a particular time, diving at a particular place. For instance, someone unfamiliar with prevailing conditions might be considered a novice diver at one dive area, but an intermediate diver at another, more familiar location.

Novice: A novice diver should be accompanied by an instructor, divemaster or advanced diver on all dives. A novice diver generally fits the following profile:
◆ basic scuba certification from an internationally recognized certifying agency
◆ dives infrequently (less than one trip a year)
◆ logged fewer than 25 total dives
◆ little or no experience diving in similar waters and conditions
◆ dives no deeper than 60ft (18m)

Intermediate: An intermediate diver generally fits the following profile:
◆ may have participated in some form of continuing diver education
◆ logged between 25 and 100 dives
◆ dives no deeper than 130ft (40m)
◆ has been diving in similar waters and conditions within the last six months

Advanced: An advanced diver generally fits the following profile:
◆ advanced certification
◆ has been diving for more than two years and logged over 100 dives
◆ has been diving in similar waters and conditions within the last six months

Regardless of your skill level, you should be in good physical condition and know your limitations. If you are uncertain of your own level of expertise for a particular site, ask the advice of a local dive instructor. He or she is best qualified to assess your abilities based on the site's prevailing dive conditions. Ultimately, however, you must decide if you are capable of making a particular dive, a decision that should take into account your level of training, recent experience and physical condition, as well as the conditions at the site. Remember that conditions can change at any time, even during a dive.

Vieques Dive Sites

The island of Vieques lies 6 miles (9.7km) east of Puerto Rico in the Vieques Passage, the waterway that separates Puerto Rico from the U.S. Virgin Islands. From the air, Vieques looks like a tropical-island movie set with crescent beaches of white sand and groves of slender palm trees. To Puerto Ricans, the island is known affectionately as La Isla Nena (Little Girl Island).

The largest of the so-called Spanish Virgin Islands, this sleepy getaway island is 20 miles (32km) long, with 9,000 residents of Taíno, Spanish, African, Danish, French, British and U.S. descent. The main town of Isabel Segunda resembles a Latin American town straight from the 1950s, right down to its old-fashioned barbershop pole. Cannons jut out from the walls of a Spanish fort that once protected this town. Country roads cross the island's rugged interior to the peaceful south shore, where the restful town of Esperanza is flanked by wedding-cake islands and sunny beaches. Since all of Vieques' dive sites lie off the south shore, divers usually find it most convenient to stay in Esperanza.

Vieques is rugged and wild and not for everybody—it's best suited for independent travelers who can drive themselves to dinner, are not afraid to explore unmarked roads and don't mind trading valet parking for a four-wheel-drive rental. Dirt roads and temporary bridges lead to dozens of truly secluded beaches,

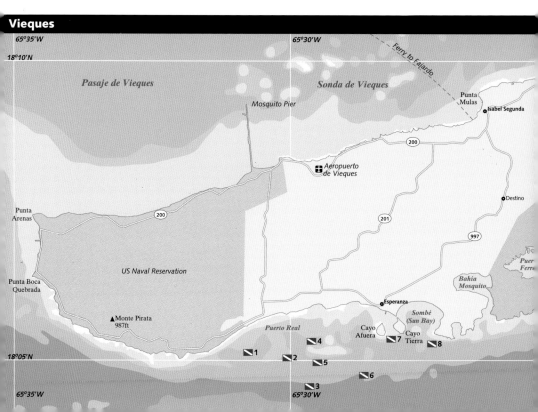

mangrove lagoons and coral reefs. Because of the U.S. naval presence, only about a third of the island is open to visitors, but a rental car is still a must.

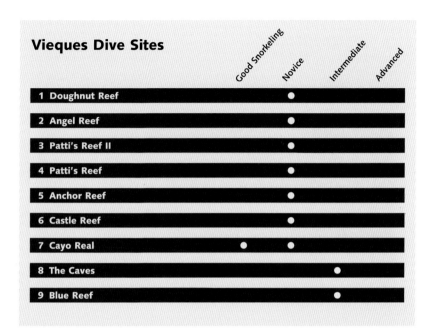

Vieques Dive Sites	Good Snorkeling	Novice	Intermediate	Advanced
1 Doughnut Reef		●		
2 Angel Reef		●		
3 Patti's Reef II		●		
4 Patti's Reef		●		
5 Anchor Reef		●		
6 Castle Reef		●		
7 Cayo Real	●	●		
8 The Caves			●	
9 Blue Reef			●	

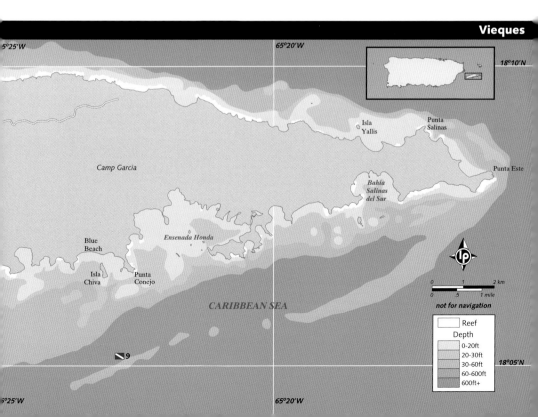

Note: It's easier and cheaper to rent a car on the island than to take it on the ferry from the Puerto Rican mainland.

While Vieques is not noted for its urban nightlife, Bahía Mosquito, a mangrove bay 2 miles (3.2km) east of Esperanza, offers a phenomenal nightly bioluminescence display. Spectators arrive in small boats or kayaks to marvel at the millions of microorganisms that give off a distinctive and ghostly blue-green glow whenever disturbed by a boat, oars or even human hands. This display occurs every night of the year but is best seen on moonless nights.

Isla Nena vs. the U.S. Navy

Vieques remains largely unspoiled by development and tourism. Somewhat ironically, this fact is probably due to the pair of U.S. Navy bases, one on each end of the island. Though there are few military personnel, the island has been used periodically since 1942 for bombing and other combat exercises. Many of the island's best beaches are on military property. These beaches are usually open to visitors, but closures occur at random to accommodate military maneuvers.

The turn of the millennium proved to be a hot time for the Navy in Vieques. In response to "No Navy" protests by island residents sparked by the accidental killing of a civilian security guard, President Clinton halted military actions on the island. Plans were reversed suddenly in early 2000, when President Clinton offered a massive increase in U.S. aid as a compromise to allow the continuation of naval activity. The future of the Navy's presence in Vieques hinges on a local referendum to be held in before March 2002. The aid increase—from US$40 million to US$90 million, amounting to some US$10,000 per Vieques resident—has sweetened the pot significantly for the island. Whether or not residents will accept the resumption of military activity before the referendum is held remains an open question. Claims that the Navy has wrought substantial environmental damage, as well as debates over the pros and cons of further tourist development, have also confused the issue significantly.

No Navy protesters occupied Isla Yallis and other parts of the island.

1   Doughnut Reef

Along the south coast of Vieques, about 30 minutes west of Esperanza by boat, lies a shallow patch reef. The coral forms an oblong reef that can be completely circumnavigated during a 50-minute dive. The white sand surrounding the reef is kept clear of seagrass by grazing marine life. From above, the site looks like a dark-blue hole ringed by a light-blue circular "doughnut" and further outlined by a ring of dark blue where the seagrass resumes growing.

From where the boat anchors, it's a shallow descent to the reef base, which is covered in swaying soft corals. Small holes in the reef are home to Caribbean spiny lobsters. This species of lobster is clawless—instead, it has an armorlike carapace fitted with sharp spines for protection. Spotted morays and the occasional green moray reside here as well.

Divers patient enough to ply the sandy bottom will be rewarded with sightings of the animated sailfin blenny. These cryptic inch-long critters occupy abandoned worm holes or similar spaces amid the

Location: 3 miles (4.8km) southwest of Esperanza

Depth Range: 20-30ft (6-9m)

Access: Boat

Expertise Rating: Novice

scattered coral debris. Look for a dark-brown or black head with blue spots around the face and neck, protruding partially out of its den. If you're lucky, you'll witness the fish's lightning-fast dash out of the hole and equally quick repeated flash or flick of its large dorsal fin. Fish experts posit that this activity communicates the blenny's whereabouts to other fish nearby. Though these blennies are not commonly seen throughout the Caribbean, they are practically a guaranteed attraction at Doughnut Reef.

Usually an easy novice dive, Doughnut Reef can be plagued with heavy surge when the trade winds blow strong from the southeast.

2   Angel Reef

A 20- or 30-minute boat ride along the south coast west of Esperanza puts you on top of Angel Reef. Since the site is about a mile offshore, dive operators use small handheld Global Positioning Systems to pinpoint its location. At Angel Reef, spur-and-groove formations run perpendicular to shore. Spur-and-groove reefs are made of long coral ridges separated by valleys of sand. They are created by wave erosion and irregular coral growth. This type of

Location: 2 miles (3.2km) southwest of Esperanza

Depth Range: 40-60ft (12-18m)

Access: Boat

Expertise Rating: Novice

reef occurs most often in shallow water near reef crests.

Two Spanish anchors can be seen here—one on the reeftop in 40ft and one at the base of the reef face in 60ft. The anchors are deeply embedded in the coral—your divemaster will usually point them out to you. The reeftop at Angel Reef is covered in gently swaying soft corals, mostly giant sea rods and lavender venus sea fans. Yellow wrasse swim quickly along the reef edge, which drops steeply to join a large white-sand channel. Schools of gray angelfish are also present here. Visibility is usually 50 to 60ft and, though the surface can be a bit bumpy, there is little or no current underwater.

3 Patti's Reef II

Southwest of Esperanza and slighty farther from shore than the original Patti's Reef, Patti's Reef II is a pleasant novice dive along a tract of boulder corals and abundant soft corals. Except during periodic wind shifts, the site is protected from cooling winter trade winds, so anchorage and entry is usually calm. Currents at Patti's Reef II are moderate or nonexistent.

The reef's dominant feature is a pair of sandy holes surrounded by hard-coral outcroppings that rise 5 to 8ft from the bottom. Massive mounds of boulder star coral (also known as mountainous star

Location: 2 miles (3.2km) southwest of Esperanza

Depth Range: 35-50ft (11-15m)

Access: Boat

Expertise Rating: Novice

coral) provide the main relief. The area is also known for its rich diversity of octo-corals, including giant split-pore sea rods. Sea rods are made up of soft, fuzzy, round, tan branches and can grow to nearly 5ft tall. Other soft coral species—such as spiny sea fans, bipinnate sea plumes and green venus sea fans—crowd the reeftop.

A diver tracks bluehead wrasse and chromis around colonies of mountainous star coral.

The profuse coral growth provides an ideal habitat for many reef tropicals. The flat boulder corals are perpetual nesting sites for mating pairs of sergeant majors. The male sergeant major defends the reddish-purple egg patches from predators like parrotfish, butterflyfish and rock beauties. The sergeant major's usual coloring is white with black stripes and a yellow upper body. When the male is tending to the egg patches, however, it enters a distinct blue-grey or brown phase. Look also for schools of yellow-and-white whiskered goatfish probing the bottom in search of food, the silent stealth of a southern stingray gliding over the sand, or even the donkey dung sea cucumber, which inhabits the sandy areas and seagrass beds around reefs.

4 Patti's Reef

Patti's Reef offers divers a sun-drenched series of sand channels within sight of the buildings of Esperanza. The channels' undersides and edges are laced with bright orange icing sponges punctuated by massive elkhorn corals and spires of boulder star coral. The more-delicate staghorn corals favor the reef's shallow top.

The base of the reef is riddled with cavities, holes and crevices that house a surprising number of inhabitants including nurse sharks, quick red-spotted hawkfish and tight schools of football-shaped doctorfish. Mackerels and other pelagics cruise in from deeper

Location: 1.5 miles (2.4km) southwest of Esperanza

Depth Range: 20-40ft (6-12m)

Access: Boat

Expertise Rating: Novice

water, while prehistoric-looking sand divers lie on the bottom with their mouths slightly open, revealing shining sharp teeth. With a flick of the tail, they disappear and settle again on the bottom close by.

The aptly named sand diver often buries itself in the sandy floor, leaving only its head visible.

The remains of a centuries-old ship anchor are barely visible under profuse encrusting coral growth.

5 Anchor Reef

This section of seafloor, 15 minutes by boat from Esperanza, makes a great novice dive. The bottom is a broad low-lying reef that spreads out in all directions. The corals here form two oddly shaped bowls, which are filled with white sand. The bowls are contained by 5- to 10ft-tall canyon walls, roughly forming an elongated figure eight with an assortment of encrusting sea life and soft corals. Look for large bar jacks, southern stingrays, crevalle jacks, barracuda on patrol and spider crabs clinging to the undersides of coral ledges.

Location: 1.5 miles (2.4km) southwest of Esperanza

Depth Range: 50-60ft (15-18m)

Access: Boat

Expertise Rating: Novice

Near one of the coral canyons rests a Spanish anchor. Once, after a visit from a main island dive club, the anchor disappeared. Weeks later, the anchor was rediscovered—in front of the errant dive club's headquarters. It was returned to the reef, upholding the site's name.

6 Castle Reef

Directly south of the Esperanza pier and just west of Cayo Real, Castle Reef is an easy dive. This low-lying reef spreads out in all directions, forming canyons with many convoluted ledges. Because the reef is shallow, you can spend a good deal of bottom time observing nature's handiwork unfold under each ledge.

Location: 1 mile (1.6km) south of Esperanza

Depth Range: 30-35ft (9-11m)

Access: Boat

Expertise Rating: Novice

The reef offers excellent fish-watching. Sharknosed gobies and other tiny ocean citizens perch on outlandish carpets of colored star corals. Yellow-and-silver lane snappers drift about. You'll also see dusky black-and-white highhats, which prefer the cover and indirect light of holes in the coral. Closely resembling highhats are spotted drums, also present at this site. Both of these black-and-white banded fish species make an unusual low beating sound by vibrating their swim bladders. Perhaps the most distinctive characteristic of the juvenile spotted drum is its long slender dorsal fin, which touches its tail fin in a graceful arch. In the seclusion of small cave entrances and beneath ledges, individuals, pairs and even trios dart about in a beautiful undersea waltz, waving their chiffon fins in the most fragile yet refined manner.

A graceful pair of juvenile spotted drums.

7 Cayo Real

No matter what your level of experience, the highlight of your trip to Vieques is likely to be the shallow shore-based snorkel trip led by underwater naturalist Captain Richard of Vieques Nature Tours (☎ 741-1980). Richard is a knowledgeable and energetic young man native to Vieques. His three-hour trip begins from the beach next to the pier in Esperanza and incorporates all the joys of floating, swimming and fish-watching, along with instruction if needed. Even experienced divers should not miss this trip.

You will begin by snorkeling around the Esperanza pier. Here you may see unusual and hard-to-find critters like seahorses, frogfish, flying gurnards, mutton hamlet and even searobins. The searobin has fins for swimming, wings for gliding, and even a set of three fingerlike appendages that act like legs for crawling. After exploring the environment beneath

Location: Off Esperanza Pier

Depth Range: 0-30ft (0-9m)

Access: Shore

Expertise Rating: Novice

the pier, you head out, finning your way across a shallow seagrass bed full of surprises unique to that particular habitat. Richard will stop to point out items of interest, explaining much about the individual behavioral characteristics of the organisms you will see.

The journey also includes the complex ecosystem surrounding the reef near the tiny island of Cayo Real. After resting for a while on shore, you'll finish the trip with a short swim back to the beach in front of Esperanza.

The rubble under Esperanza's pier is home to unusual critters like flying gurnards and seahorses.

See Horses?

Two seahorse species—longsnout and lined—are found in the Caribbean. These small delicate-looking fish prefer shallow waters and can be seen along Puerto Rico's north coast and in shallow shore dives like Vieques' Cayo Real. In the same family (*Syngnathidae*) as pipefish, the seahorse's delicate body resembles the chess knight. They use their prehensile tails to grasp rope sponges, seagrass and other holdfasts. Unlike pipefish and most other fish, which swim horizontally, seahorses swim upright, using only their dorsal and pectoral fins.

Seahorses are usually well camouflaged—they deploy a combination of color, texture and motion to remain largely undetected by predators. They use their horselike snouts to feed on planktonic crustaceans. The breeding habits of the seahorse are an especially noteworthy feature of the animal. The female gives the eggs to the male to be incubated in his pouch for about six weeks. The male often rubs or scratches his pouch against other objects to encourage the youngsters out. With this stimulation, as many as 300 tiny seahorses disperse and immediately begin to feed.

8 The Caves

East of Esperanza, a long, narrow peninsula called Cayo Tierra (Land Cay) forms the western boundary of Sombé (also called Sun Bay). From afar Cayo Tierra appears to be an island, but it is actually a low-lying spit connected to the mainland. The sandy spit is an excellent area for beach-combing. Near the end of Cayo Tierra is a shallow, surgy dive site called The Caves. Visibility is poor, usually 30ft or less, and you should expect moderate to heavy surge action.

Location: Off Cayo Tierra

Depth Range: 25-35ft (7.5-11m)

Access: Boat

Expertise Rating: Intermediate

This area was once a majestic hard-coral reef sporting huge colonies of elkhorn corals, but many were destroyed by hurricanes and heavy storms. You'll see the remains of giant branches of elkhorn corals lying like fallen trees in healthy fields of swaying swollen-knob candelabrum corals.

The site's many caves have been sculpted by sand carried on the power-ful oceanic surge. Divers taking refuge inside these caves can expect to see nurse sharks gently resting on the sand. Uncommon and reclusive, the reef croaker hides in the caves during the day, emerging only to feed at night. In the same family as the drum, croakers are dark and silver with large eyes. If you are patient enough to allow your eyes to adjust to the dim light of the recesses, you may be rewarded with a sighting of this fish, which is rare in this part of Caribbean.

9 Blue Reef

About 6 miles east of Esperanza, Blue Reef is found along some of the prettiest shoreline Vieques has to offer. Traveling along the Caribbean coast by boat, buffeted by the fresh trade winds, you'll pass the entrance to phosphorescent Bahía Mosquito and you'll even catch a glimpse of the defunct lighthouse at Puerto Ferro. Much of this section of coastline consists of yellow-gold layered sandstone cliffs that spill into long, sweeping white-sand beaches.

Blue Reef rises out of a mixed sand and rock bottom at 80ft. Oddly enough, the dropoff faces the shore. This gigantic reef stretches east to west for more than 2 miles and much of the area remains unexplored. Divers are usually greeted with the best visibility in Vieques—about 60 to 100ft. Because the crystal-blue water generates moderate to strong currents, this dive is best done as a drift dive. The irregular reef face forms a number of steep ledges that begin in 60 to 70ft and drop to 80ft. Blue Reef is far

Location: 2 miles (3.2km) south of Blue Beach

Depth Range: 60-80ft (18-24m)

Access: Boat

Expertise Rating: Intermediate

enough from shore that it can be quite rough on the surface, even on an average day.

At 80ft, this dive is deep enough that you should expect to experience a mild thermocline—the sea temperature usually drops 3°F (1.7°C) or more as you approach the bottom. Appropriate exposure protection is recommended. Though your bottom time will be shorter than on shallower dives, you'll still have enough time to see a variety of oddly shaped sponges, including branching vase sponges, giant barrel sponges and rope sponges.

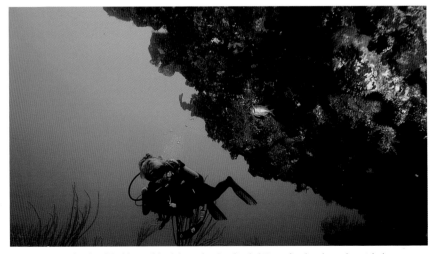

During the day, blackbar soldierfish prefer the dim lighting of a deeply undercut ledge.

Culebra Dive Sites

In the Vieques Passage, halfway between Puerto Rico and St. Thomas, Culebra is part of the chain of islands forming the geographical boundary of the Caribbean Sea. Geologically, Culebra is more a part of the Virgin Islands than of mainland Puerto Rico.

Easily accessed by plane from San Juan and Fajardo or by ferry from Fajardo, Culebra is an idyllic weekend retreat for Puerto Ricans looking to leave behind the fast pace of San Juan. Dewey, the island's main community, is very small—it never takes more than 10 minutes to walk from one place to another. Culebra has no traffic lights, no movie theaters and no large hotels. Instead, modest guest houses and restaurants line the small canals that transform this charming tropical island into the Venice of the Caribbean.

The pace here is markedly slower and more rural than the rest of Puerto Rico. When you get to Culebra, be prepared for things to be done a little differently. Realize that a restaurant owner may open her doors only when she is in the mood, and don't be put off if your favorite breakfast place is out of pastries because the baker went kayaking.

Beyond the casual nature of the culture, Culebra's most endearing charms are its natural resources. You could snorkel, kayak, hike, fish or sail here every day for a year and still not feel like you had "done" Culebra. Luckily, much of the island—including all of the coastline and the offshore cays—is protected as part the Culebra National Wildlife Reserve, and development of the interior is heavily restricted. That said, none of the dive sites covered in this book lie within the actual boundaries of the reserve.

The beaches at Culebrita attract snorkelers as well as sea turtles, which lay eggs here in summer.

For locals, the sea is a way of life. Many residents commute to work in motorized boats or dinghies. For visitors, the white-sand beaches, clear water and miles of coral reef are the island's main attractions. The smaller islands and cays around Culebra provide a variety of conditions and environments suitable for divers and snorkelers of all levels. Culebra's waters explode with populations of colorful reef fish like nowhere else in Puerto Rico.

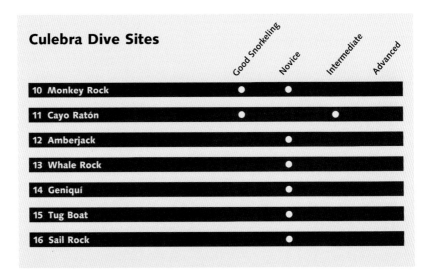

Culebra Dive Sites

	Good Snorkeling	Novice	Intermediate	Advanced
10 Monkey Rock	●	●		
11 Cayo Ratón	●		●	
12 Amberjack		●		
13 Whale Rock		●		
14 Geniquí		●		
15 Tug Boat		●		
16 Sail Rock		●		

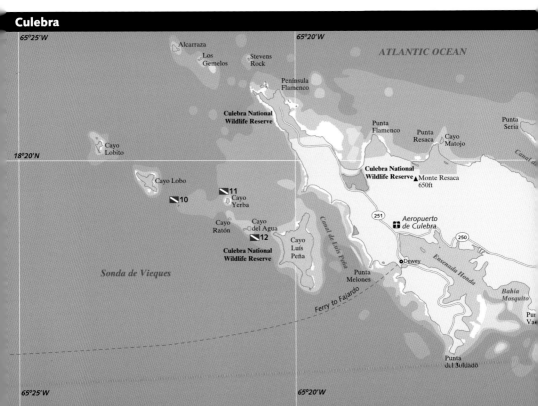

Culebra

10 Monkey Rock

West of Culebra, past Cayo Yerba, is the low-lying Monkey Rock. Divers usually explore its protected west side. A series of large boulders leads down to the sand. Though currents can pick up at times, Monkey Rock is a good site for divers and snorkelers looking for a slow swim through a gardenlike environment.

Location: .5 miles (.8km) west of Cayo Yerba

Depth Range: 15-55ft (4.5-17m)

Access: Boat

Expertise Rating: Novice

The rocks are adorned with soft corals, sponges and tunicates all in purple, orange, pink, red and green. Huge schools of bright-red bigeye drift by, numbering as many as 100 individuals. You'll also find clusters of reef butterflyfish. Strange armored slipper lobsters cling to the rock inside cracks and crevices. Close inspection may reveal golden-tailed morays poking out of holes in the rock. Large schools of silver sennet— members of the barracuda family that grow to only about 18 inches—often will encircle a diver. These fish pose no threat to your safety.

Reef butterflyfish.

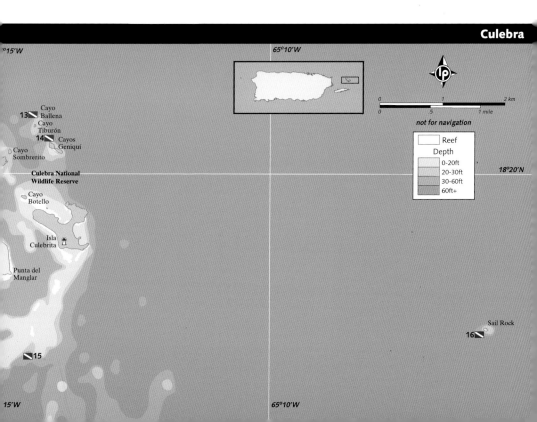

Culebra

65°10'W

65°10'W

°15'W

15'W

18°20'N

0   1   2 km
0   .5   1 mile

not for navigation

13   Cayo Ballena
  Cayo Tiburón
14   Cayos Geniquí
Cayo Sombrerito

Culebra National Wildlife Reserve

Cayo Botello

Isla Culebrita

Punta del Manglar

15

Sail Rock

16

Reef
Depth
0-20ft
20-30ft
30-60ft
60ft+

11 Cayo Ratón

One of the 20 or more rocks and islands west of Culebra, Cayo Ratón (meaning Rat Cay) is the best site west of Culebra for fish-watching. Boats anchor in a small rock cove on the cay's north side. Underwater, a flat plateau at 20 to 30ft extends about 50 yards from shore, where it slopes steeply to 50ft.

The reef buzzes with fish life. Schooling horse-eye jacks spiral over the reef plateau. Speedy bonnetfish zoom in and out of view and brilliant spotfin butterflyfish swim around the lacy sea fans. Yellow and orange crinoids reach out from cracks in the reef. Large numbers of magnificent queen angelfish and parrotfish parade by. Watch for the unusual-looking peacock flounder, which stares up from the sand with a pair of

Location: Just north of Cayo Ratón

Depth Range: 20-50ft (6-15m)

Access: Boat

Expertise Rating: Intermediate

radar eyes that move independently from one another.

The large schools of fish make for good wide-angle photo opportunities while the assortment and abundance of reef fish in general make this a productive place for fish portraits. Visibility averages 50 to 75ft and can easily exceed 100ft on a good day. Currents can be quite strong.

Successful Fish-Watching

The key to successful fish-watching is to expand your underwater global awareness. Slow down and look all around you, not just in front of you. Turn around, look up and even look behind you. Settle into a relaxed, comfortable rate of breathing. Take the time to fine-tune your buoyancy—with each inhalation, you should feel yourself begin to rise slightly, and as you exhale, you'll slowly sink back down.

The reef's smaller creatures invite closer observation. While the standard fare of tropical reef fish can be seen swimming over the coral or sandy bottom, many other intriguing critters prefer to remain hidden under ledges or may blend in so well with their surroundings that you'll miss them if you swim too quickly.

Encounters with large marine life are certainly exciting, but you won't be lucky on every dive. To ensure a rewarding dive each time, you'll have to search for the smaller reef inhabitants. Explore habitats that you may have overlooked in the past, such as seagrass beds or large areas of sand or rock rubble. It's rewarding to see the bizarre creatures that have evolved adapted traits for their particular habitats. It's useful to learn to distinguish fish characteristics by knowing, for example, the difference between a pectoral fin and a ventral fin. Best of all, share each new find with a buddy and use the extra pair of eyes to look for ever more amazing discoveries.

Once you have an increased awareness of your surroundings, listen to your senses. When your sixth sense whispers to you, turn around and look behind you—you might be surprised to see what is watching you. Each dive comes with plenty to enjoy, it's up to you to make the most of it!

12 Amberjack

Amberjack lies west of Dewey, near the many grass-covered rocky islands that decorate the waters in this area. The site is named for the many schooling silver amberjacks, which keep in tight fighter formation and face into the current.

Out of the profusion of tan-colored soft corals near the bottom, tiny black-and-yellow striped wrasse set up cleaning stations to rid larger fish, including barracuda, of unwanted parasites. A family of large French angelfish glides over a long line of rocks smothered in delicate sponges and deepwater gorgonians. At the end of the row of rocks is an enormous boulder jutting way up off the

Location: West of Cayo Luis Peña

Depth Range: 50-60ft (15-18m)

Access: Boat

Expertise Rating: Intermediate

flat sand bottom in about 60ft of water. Photographers can easily spend the entire dive circling the rock examining the wealth of subjects and scenes for wide-angle or macro. Visibility at Amberjack averages 50 to 60ft and currents range from mild to strong.

French angelfish usually travel in pairs and are relatively unafraid of divers.

13 Whale Rock

Whale Rock (Cayo Ballena in Spanish) is just off the northeast perimeter of the small ring of rocks and cays that surrounds Culebra. Here a low-lying arch of volcanic black stone is stripped bare of vegetation by winter storms, which send water crashing up into the air and onto the rock. At times the rock looks like an enormous humpback whale splashing down after a full breech, earning the rock its name. Seabirds enjoy the isolation of Whale Rock and, underwater, marine life clings to its sides.

In some places the rock's sides drop vertically. Elsewhere, the undersea hill melts down to depths around 90ft. At any depth you can work on partially circumnavigating this inside-out aquarium of reef fish, invertebrates and coral. Whale Rock is like a fish magnet. Large schools of bar jacks and yellowtail snappers fill the water column as they circle through the seascape. Families of gray angelfish

Location: .5 miles (.8km) northeast of Cayo Norte

Depth Range: 30-90ft (9-27m)

Access: Boat

Expertise Rating: Intermediate

nibble at sponges. The west side of the rock is perhaps the best part of this site, where the tapestry of color is a photographer's dream.

Heavy surge and strong currents often send divers elsewhere for the day's first dive. However, most dive operators will bring you to Whale Rock any chance they get. Though water conditions are generally less favorable from November through April, there are plenty of days throughout the year when divers can enjoy Whale Rock.

Deepwater gorgonians and orange cup corals are fostered by nutrient-rich tidal currents.

14 Geniquí

A short distance east of Whale Rock, Geniquí (pronounced henny-KEY) makes for an excellent second dive of the day. The site's most notable features are the large swell-carved tunnels, canyons and caves. These are among the largest saltwater caves that divers can explore in Puerto Rico. The tops of the caves are covered with blossoming colonies of orange cup corals. The caves are also home to schools of nocturnal fish such as glassy sweepers, bigeyes and cardinalfish. The caves are not very long—when inside, you'll never be far from the entrance or exit—so, while an underwater light is nice to have, it's certainly not mandatory.

As with other sites north of Culebra, conditions at Geniquí can be rough. (If you've already made the Whale Rock

Location: .8 miles (1.3km) east of Cayo Norte

Depth Range: 20-50ft (6-15m)

Access: Boat

Expertise Rating: Intermediate

dive, then conditions should be sufficiently calm.) A word of warning: Do not dive Geniquí if there is a north swell. The swell can be deceptive, as there may be a long series of small waves followed by two or three big ones. Rest assured that dive operators from Culebra won't take you to these sites unless the conditions are acceptable.

A diver explores the large swell-carved caves and surge channels at Geniquí.

15 Tug Boat

The area east of Culebra boasts many small shallow reefs that come within striking distance of the surface, making boat navigation difficult. On a calm day, a tug boat from the West Indian Transport Company ran hard aground atop a small reef about 2 miles from the entrance to Hurricane Hole, a southeast-facing bay in Culebra. The crew remained on board for

Location: .8 miles (1.3km) southeast of Punta Vaca

Depth Range: 10-30ft (3-9m)

Access: Boat

Expertise Rating: Intermediate

Most of Tug Boat is easy to explore, but only trained wreck divers should venture deep inside.

days to offload what they could, then abandoned her. After other boats suffered similar accidents by mistakenly following the tug, the Coast Guard pulled the wreck off the reef and sunk her. In September 1989, Hurricane Hugo disturbed the tug, moving it to where she now rests, not far from her original grounding spot.

Today, the wreck rests in her shallow grave within sight of the lighthouse on the small island of Culebrita. Her bow is nestled into the base of one of the area's reefs. Because the site is shallow, the surge can be heavy on rough days. Tug Boat is best dived during the calmer summer months (May to October). The wreck itself is impressively intact and corals are beginning to grow on the deck and inside the ship's interior. The wheelhouse is open and relatively easy to explore, but the hatches and below-deck areas leading to the engine room are best left to divers trained in wreck diving.

Look in this area for vast fields of staghorn coral. The area's steep-walled reefs prove interesting to several varieties of territorial damselfish, while large numbers of striped sergeant majors prefer the better-oxygenated shallow waters of the reeftop. Tug Boat allows ample bottom time for exploring, and visibility is good—averaging 60 to 75ft—so photographers will be rewarded with classic wreck shots in sunny water.

16 Sail Rock

Five miles out to sea lies the ghostly uninhabited shape of Sail Rock. Entirely white with guano, Sail Rock towers to 125ft, serving as a beacon for divers from as far away as Fajardo, Vieques and even St. John in the U.S. Virgin Islands. Although Sail Rock is just 6 miles southwest of St. Thomas and is considered part of the U.S. Virgin Islands, it is most frequented by divers departing from Culebra.

Location: 5.3 miles (8.5km) east of Punta Vaca

Depth Range: 30-90ft (9-27m)

Access: Boat

Expertise Rating: Intermediate

This is an ideal multi-level dive. Start by descending to 90ft and explore the base of any of the three pinnacles. From there, ascend to 60ft, continuing to circumnavigate the towering rock before again slowly coming up to 30ft to finish the dive. Take special care when moving from one pinnacle to the next so you don't inadvertently descend deeper than you planned.

Below the surface, Sail Rock is nothing short of a high-voltage dive. The water is unbelievably clear and is filled with rich colors and detail. You may see several turtles on a single dive, Caribbean reef sharks are a common sight, and you'll likely see at least one other pelagic, such as wahoo. Look for great barracuda demonstrating many types of behavior, such as schooling, camouflaging and hunting. You might also catch sight of the black-and-blue midnight parrotfish, which can grow to 3ft long—it is considered somewhat rare in this part of the Caribbean.

About 160ft west of Sail Rock, you'll encounter three fantastically tall pinnacles buzzing with schooling creole wrasse, blue chromis and black durgons. You'll also see Nassau, tiger and black groupers, which biologists consider an indicator of the healthiest reef ecosystems. The trio of pinnacles stand close together and are covered from top to bottom with living marine organisms. Most notable are the large colorful odd-shaped sponges like strawberry vase sponges, bright orange elephant ear sponges and rough-textured azure vase sponges.

All this excitement does come with a price, however, as conditions at Sail Rock can be rough with heavy surge. Proper planning is important to avoid the strongest currents and all divers should carry safety sausages.

Marine life covers the Sail Rock pinnacles from top to bottom, making it the area's best dive.

Fajardo Dive Sites

The northeast is one of Puerto Rico's most convenient dive regions for residents and visitors based out of San Juan. The island's northeast point is linked by an undersea plateau with the Virgin Islands to the east. Most of the region's diving takes place around the small offshore islands and cays, especially the islands of Diablo, Lobos, Palominos and the smaller Palomenitos.

Dive operators from as far south as Humacao and as far west as Bayomón escort divers to the northeast reefs. Locally, many dive boats leave from near the marina at El Conquistador Resort in Las Croabas, which is ideally situated close to the islands extending east from Las Cabezas de San Juan.

The landscape west of Fajardo is dominated by the mountains of the El Yunque rainforest. Each year, millions of gallons of freshwater runoff find their way down to the coast, reducing underwater visibility near shore. Luckily, the

The resort-run Palominos Island offers watersports, horseback riding and a beautiful beach.

outer cays are located just outside the greenish band of water near shore, so visibility is improved. The topography underwater is largely fringing reefs, patch reefs and spur-and-groove formations, and there are many good snorkeling sites in this region.

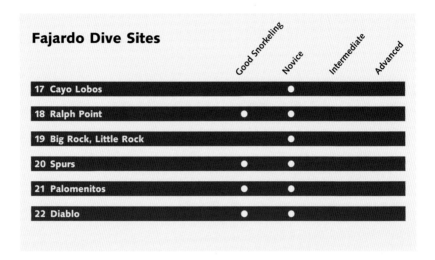

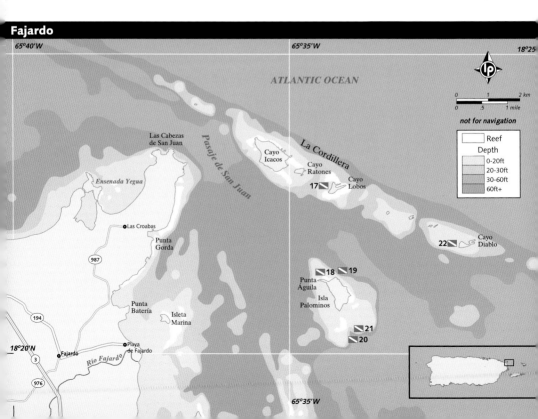

17 Cayo Lobos

Cayo Lobos (Wolves Cay) is one of the northernmost small cays off northeast Puerto Rico. This dive site is loaded with caves, tunnels and archways ranging from just below the surface to 30ft, making it an excellent second or third dive of the day. Divers exploring the area are dwarfed by enormous rounded mounds of boulder star corals. Many smaller leaf, plate and sheet corals make up the porous outlines of the reef. Tightly packed schools of blue tangs patrol for good grazing grounds, swimming through the brilliant shafts of sunlight that penetrate from the surface. Small sharpnosed puffers—the underwater version of a hummingbird—flit about, turning on a dime.

At night the scene changes to include some zany crustaceans, eels searching for meals, and flowering corals. The corals' gelatinous polyps serve to trap squiggly worms, which explode on contact with the polyps. Peer beneath just about any ledge and dozens of pairs of reflective eyes belonging to red night or peppermint shrimp will stare right back at you.

At daybreak, the nocturnal creatures head for the reef's darkest recesses and the parrotfish swim free of their nightly mucous cocoons to resume their habitual pecking at the reef. When feeding, parrotfish use their fused "beaks" to scrape algae off the corals. Parrotfish are the

Location: Just west of Cayo Lobos

Depth Range: 3-30ft (1-9m)

Access: Boat

Expertise Rating: Novice

crop dusters of the Caribbean—in the grazing process, the fish ingest some of the coral itself, which is then excreted as sand.

Lettuce coral grows in colonies, forming a series of thick upright lobes.

18 Ralph Point

Ralph Point is an excellent novice dive that begins just 10ft below the surface. Divers will find plenty to explore as the reef's varied structure offers lots of relief. The reef joins the sandy bottom in a series of S-curves formed by the reef's many coral bowls and mounds. The bottom doesn't fall below 60ft and the average depth is about 40 to 50ft. Ralph Point can be an excellent spot for snorkeling.

Location: Off northwest point of Isla Palominos

Depth Range: 10-60ft (3-18m)

Access: Boat

Expertise Rating: Novice

Most of the common reef fish are found here, including parrotfish, sergeant majors, trumpetfish and many goby and blenny species. The silty sand bottom at the reef edge is a favorite habitat for mantis shrimp. You'll need a sharp eye to find the sculpted burrow of a scaly-tailed mantis—the largest of the mantis shrimp species in the Caribbean—along the flat, sandy bottom.

With large, double-lobed eyes, these crustaceans somewhat resemble the terrestrial praying mantis insect. The mantis shrimp is an ambush predator that relies heavily on concealment, burrowing into perfectly cylindrical vertical shafts in the sand. It lies waiting in its burrow, with only its radar eyes peering up through a fine layer of sand. When a fish enters the general vicinity of the lair, the shrimp suddenly bursts through the sand to grab the unsuspecting prey with fast, snapping claws armed with razor-sharp spines.

Known to Caribbean fishermen as "thumbsplitters," mantis shrimp are aggressive if molested, and their claws can inflict deep and painful gashes. If you're cautious, the mantis shrimp can be safely observed from a close range, but be careful where you rest your hands in the sand. Mantis shrimp burrows are usually found in the flat sandy areas close to the reef edge.

The mantis shrimp relies on ambush techniques to feed itself.

19 Big Rock, Little Rock

Along the rocky north side of the off-shore island of Palominos, near a large red buoy, you'll find a dive site called Big Rock, Little Rock. Here, a fringing reef extends from Palominos, roughly following the contour of the island. Dense stony corals such as grooved brain corals and rough cactus corals provide much of the reef's structure. You'll find the best coral cover along the sloping reef face, where you might catch sight of an eagle ray. There are also many oval-shaped patch reefs scattered over the sandy bottom at 50 to 60ft. Because Big Rock, Little Rock is on the protected lee side of the island, you'll notice more delicate staghorn and finger corals than you'll find at the unprotected windward sites. Visibility around the island is generally less than 60ft.

Location: Just northwest of Palominos

Depth Range: 30-60ft (9-18m)

Access: Boat

Expertise Rating: Novice

Look for gobies running their cleaning stations. Cleaning gobies lie atop the coral heads, showing off their distinctive blue and yellow stripes to the potential customers, the larger fish that cruise in to be cleaned of unwanted parasites. In exchange for its efforts, the cleaner goby gets a good meal. This mutually beneficial association is just one of many symbiotic relationships in the reef environment.

Groomers of the Sea

Observant divers will discover a variety of symbiotic relationships—associations in which two dissimilar organisms participate in a mutually beneficial relationship—throughout the marine world. One of the most interesting symbiotic relationships is found at cleaning stations, where one animal advertises its grooming services to potential clients with a series of inviting undulating movements.

Cleaner species include gobies, wrasse, shrimp, angelfish, butterflyfish and tangs. One of the most common cleaners in Puerto Rico is the cleaning goby. These tiny fish have a blue-and-white striped body with a yellow V on their heads. They swarm all over the stony corals waiting for fish to approach their protected area of the reef. Once a fish makes the appropriate sig-

STEVE ROSENBERG

A tiger grouper gets a cleaning from an eager pair of gobies.

nals to be cleaned, the gobies remove debris, decaying skin and infection from all available surfaces, including the inside of a customer's mouth and gills. When danger approaches the fish will close its mouth and gills, but still leave enough room for the gobies to exit the much larger fish and retreat to safety. Although the customer could have an easy snack, it would never swallow the essential cleaner. The large fish benefits from the removal of parasites and dead tissue, while the little cleaner is provided with a "free" meal.

20 Spurs

Spurs is one of several dives around the idyllic deserted island of Palomenitos. Boat charters from Las Croabas' El Conquistador Resort or Fajardo travel 30 or 40 minutes to the island's southeast side. The site's name comes from the long spur-and-groove reef that runs north to south. Beginning in the shallows, divers navigate through canyons ("grooves") carved in the coral. The steep walls of the "spurs" slope from 20 or 30ft down to 60ft.

The iron remains of a small shipwreck lie in about 70ft in a sandy area near the reef. The wreck is home to schools of goatfish, giant sea anemones, arrow crabs, spotted lobsters and banded coral shrimp. Though the wreck itself is not worthy of an entire dive, it does make a nice addition to the natural wonders of the reef.

Here, as at all dives near Palomenitos or the larger Palominos island, be sure to keep an eye on the blue water for silent gliding giant pelagics. Spurs is

Location: Southeast of Palomenitos

Depth Range: 20-70ft (6-21m)

Access: Boat

Expertise Rating: Novice

probably the best spot off Puerto Rico to see spotted eagle rays, among the most impressive of coral reef inhabitants. This ray habitually cruises along the bottom in search of prey, using its long tongue to probe the sand for shellfish. These large creatures are sometimes accompanied by remoras, also called sharksuckers. This pesky fish uses a flat, oval-shaped sucker on top of its head to ride along with its host, cleaning up any scraps of food left behind by the ray. Occasionally you'll see an eagle ray leap as much as 5ft clear of the water. Some experts say that the ray is trying to rid itself of these unwanted guests.

It's easy to figure out how the giant brain coral earned its groovy name.

21 Palomenitos

Palominos island and its tiny neighbor island Palomenitos lie offshore of Fajardo. The shallow, patterned reef surrounding deserted Palomenitos is excellent for both snorkeling and diving as it is quite close to shore. This dive is an easy walk in the park and good for many frames to the underwater photographer.

Location: Just southeast of Palomenitos

Depth Range: 20-60ft (6-18m)

Access: Boat

Expertise Rating: Novice

The reef face is adorned with numerous sea fans, sea whips and sea plumes. Out in the sandy areas within sight of the fringing reef, look for the eyes of southern stingrays buried under a camouflage of sand.

Occasional glances away from the reef may reveal giant eagle rays as they glide by silently. Also look for hawksbill turtles resting on the bottom amid tangles of soft coral.

Sponges and soft and hard corals form an unusual patterned reef.

22 Diablo

Cayo Diablo (Devil Cay) is one of a chain of small, low-lying islands that stretches away from the mainland's northeastern Cabezas de San Juan. This prized site is a favorite of local dive clubs and operators, so divers are likely to see other boats in the area. The cay has a beautiful beach and the shallow areas are great for snorkeling. Since currents can run strong, you should always try to start the dive moving upcurrent from the boat, making your return safer and easier.

Location: 4 miles (6.4km) east of Cabezas de San Juan

Depth Range: 15-50ft (4.5-15m)

Access: Boat

Expertise Rating: Novice

This predominantly hard-coral reef looks like a well-manicured garden.

Great barracuda watch over divers curiously, while large formations of yellow-and-white goatfish and hundreds of dazzling blue chromis stay near the reef. Look for fan-shaped amber pen-shells in a variety of habitats—they may be buried in the sand or tucked away in the reef's narrow openings.

On the boat ride from San Juan or Fajardo, look for dolphins. In one very unusual encounter, divers saw a lone West Indian manatee that had wandered miles out to sea from its usual coastal mangrove habitat. The sea cow, as manatees are commonly called, was slow-moving and easy to approach. Once abundant off the south coast, manatee populations in Puerto Rico and throughout the Caribbean have been threatened by the depletion of mangrove areas.

A group of striking neon-blue chromis flashes through a convoluted reefscape.

Humacao Dive Sites

Diving the southeast region of Puerto Rico means departing from the marina at the Palmas del Mar resort, about 3 miles (4.8km) southwest of the city of Humacao. Cooling ocean breezes mingle with tall slender palm trees along a golden-sand beach lapped by warm waves. This is one of the island's main nesting areas for green and hawksbill turtles. Guests staying at the resort have witnessed the miraculous sight of hundreds of turtle hatchlings popping up out of the sand and quickly scuttling their way down to the sea.

Around the main island, underwater visibility improves dramatically just a few miles offshore.

Because wind-driven waves and large amounts of freshwater runoff compromise water clarity near shore, southeast dive sites tend to be well away from shore. As you travel to the dive sites, you'll notice that the skirt of greenish water gives way to the deeper, clearer blues. Only two operators dive out of the Humacao region—both have boats that depart from the marina at the Palmas del Mar resort.

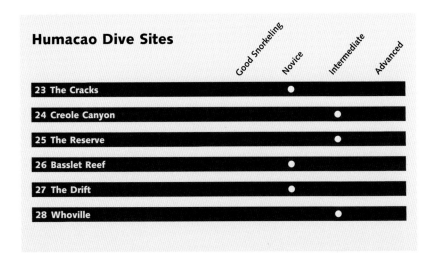

Humacao Dive Sites	Good Snorkeling	Novice	Intermediate	Advanced
23 The Cracks		●		
24 Creole Canyon			●	
25 The Reserve			●	
26 Basslet Reef		●		
27 The Drift		●		
28 Whoville			●	

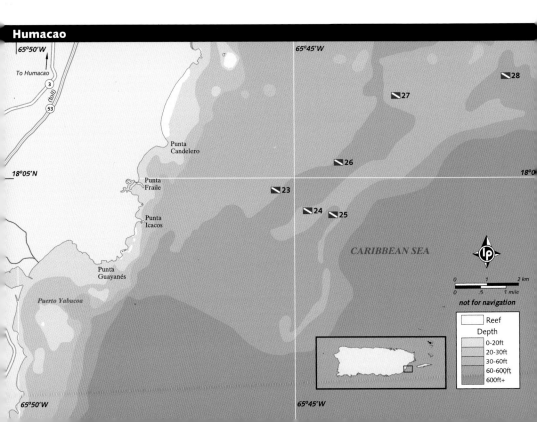

23 The Cracks

This often-visited spot lies less than 10 minutes by boat from the marina at Palmas del Mar. The main difference between The Cracks and sites farther offshore is that the visibility here is normally not as good—in the 30 to 60ft range.

Location: 3 miles (4.8km) southeast of Palmas del Mar resort

Depth Range: 50-70ft (15-21m)

Access: Boat

Expertise Rating: Novice

Despite the poorer visibility, divers are attracted to this site by the unique topography. The base of this inshore reef has eroded away over time, creating trenches, ledges and overhangs that come together to form arches and tunnels. The sides of these ledges are loaded with dazzling purple-and-orange fairy basslets and blackbar soldierfish. From the top, divers can only be detected by their bubbles percolating up through the porous coral.

Debris loosened by exhaled bubbles and careless fins can cause unwanted backscatter for photographers using a flash and wide-angle lenses, so you'll find that your first pass under the overhangs is generally the most productive for clear pictures. Another option is to stick to macro.

At The Cracks divers spend most of their time exploring under large overhangs.

24 Creole Canyon

As you travel the several miles offshore from the Palmas del Mar resort to Creole Canyon, the green water close to shore gives way to the alluring blues of the Caribbean Sea. Underwater, this impressive miniwall drops from a soft-coral carpet on top, revealing a dark-red wall of sponges and deepwater lace corals. Mild currents bathe a subsea terrain of

Location: 3.5 miles (5.6km) southeast of Palmas del Mar resort

Depth Range: 45-80ft (14-24m)

Access: Boat

Expertise Rating: Intermediate

canyons and sand valleys. The initial descent to 45ft is an easy one and the dive averages 60 to 75ft. Visibility in this area is quite good.

Large schools of purple and orange creole wrasse swim in and out of the scene. Divers are also quite likely to see individual longsnout butterflyfish. These small triangular butterflyfish are yellow, brown and white and have adapted long, slender mouths that can reach far into coral crevices to feed on marine invertebrates.

Lace corals orient their fans into the current to comb the most nutrients out of the water.

25 The Reserve

Nearly 5 miles offshore from the Palmas del Mar resort lies this undisturbed tract of reef. As you travel farther southeast from shore the shallow reefs give way to deep reefs and walls characteristic of the south and southwest. Visibility at The Reserve is exceptionally clear, ranging from 75 to 100ft, but rough seas mean that divers prone to seasickness should take proper precautions for the boat ride out and back.

Underwater, the dark shapes of the reef rise up from a sandy bottom. The tops of these rounded hills of coral are in 60 to 70ft, while the sandy channels running farther out to sea lie in 80 to 90ft.

Location: 4.5 miles (7.2km) southeast of Palmas del Mar resort

Depth Range: 60-90ft (18-27m)

Access: Boat

Expertise Rating: Intermediate

The concentration of invertebrates and small reef fish at this site is quite impressive. Bright clumps of orange elephant ear and other sponges paint the bottom in a wild assembly of colors. Schools of striped Atlantic spadefish make you feel like you're in a huge fish tank. Look for gray angelfish nipping at divers' bubbles. This behavior makes it easy to get in close for some exciting photographs.

Gray angelfish have developed the playful habit of nipping at divers' bubbles.

26 Basslet Reef

Though Basslet Reef is too close to shore to have excellent visibility, it does have a higher density of sea life than most sites along the eastern shore of Puerto Rico. This terraced reef structure offers intriguing canyons with overhangs. The overwhelming abundance of deepwater sea fans bunched tightly together form a reddish background for schools of yellow French grunts, squirrelfish and soldierfish.

The site's boulders and dark crevices form a dramatic seascape loaded with colorful and strange creatures, such as the three-rowed sea cucumber. This

Location: 3.5 miles (5.6km) east of Palmas del Mar resort

Depth Range: 40-60ft (12-18m)

Access: Boat

Expertise Rating: Novice

echinoderm—in the same family as sea stars and sea urchins—has three rows of hundreds of small tubefeet (called podia) that work in unison to allow the animal to move and capture food. Look

Basslet Reef's terraced seascape is loaded with a remarkably high density of marine life.

for sea cucumbers lying on or slowly crawling along the bottom, feeding on organic matter in the sand.

Many small colorful fish inhabit the undersides of ledges and overhangs. The reef's terraces—which are like stone steps—provide a suitable habitat for both fairy and candy basslets. Candy basslets have yellow and maroon stripes and resemble peppermint bass. Larger fish like Atlantic spadefish and bright-yellow porkfish are other regulars at this site, and peacock flounders lie in the sand. Look for large porcupinefish, which are heavily armored with sharp spines to defend against predators, even sharks.

27 The Drift

At The Drift, a line of colorful coral ledges and some foxhole swim-throughs create shaded areas reeling with goatfish, squirrelfish and highhats. Visibility in the area is spectacular—as much as 100ft—and the reef is easily navigated.

Marine creatures abound at this site. Look for thumbnail-size flamingo tongue snails clinging to the base of the yellow, green and purple sea fans. Some marine creatures associated with night dives, such as reef squid, octopus and lobsters, are often out at this site during daylight hours as well. Almost every undersea creature enjoys the taste of octopus, so octopus have evolved into masters of camouflage and are supreme contortionists, fashioning cracks and crevices into protective dens. So if you happen to see a pile of neatly cleaned shells in front of a hole of just the right size, it probably means that an octopus was there recently.

Location: 4.5 miles (7.2km) northeast of Palmas del Mar resort

Depth Range: 45-60ft (14-18m)

Access: Boat

Expertise Rating: Novice

A venus sea fan's netlike branches comb nutrients from the water.

28 Whoville

Because of this site's unusual topography, it was named after the town in Dr. Seuss' children's book, *How the Grinch Stole Christmas*. In this Caribbean Whoville, a large teardrop-shaped coral pillar rises from the center of an incredible underwater amphitheater of coral formations. These coral structures rise from the bottom at 70ft to form bunches of miniwalls,

Location: 6.5 miles (10km) northeast of Palmas del Mar Resort

Depth Range: 50-70ft (15-21m)

Access: Boat

Expertise Rating: Intermediate

which ascend to 50ft. The undersides of these walls are crowded with orange cup corals, red rope sponges and orange ball sponges.

Small holes in the reef are sometimes full of fairy basslets. Longsnout butterflyfish flit about here, and it is also a choice location for southern stingrays and great barracuda. The sunny reeftops are packed with tan soft corals and lavender sea fans, while the side of the reef that faces the slight current bustles with blue and brown chromis. French and gray angelfish and even tiger grouper and Nassau grouper add to the cast of characters.

Whoville lies more than 6 miles east of the Palmas del Mar resort. The visibility in this area is unbelievably clear—about 100ft—but because it is in open ocean, the surface is somewhat rough at times.

The longsnout butterflyfish uses its pointed nose to root up its prey.

La Parguera Dive Sites

In contrast to the lush tropical vegetation of the north, the southern region is mostly made up of vast, dry savannahs of yellow grass and green rolling hills dotted with shade trees. Dive sites along the south coast are concentrated in the southwest, near Guánica and the small fishing village of La Parguera, off a coastal area of mangrove lagoons and sandy beaches.

On weekends and holidays, the small fishing village of La Parguera fills with visitors plying the area's endless canals. The calm lagoon waterways are lined with colorfully painted houseboats and homes built on stilts. The seemingly floating islands of mangrove trees provide a unique ecology and nursery for all types of reef fish. La Parguera's big draw, however, is the nightly show at nearby Bahía Fosforente. This bioluminescent bay is one of a handful in Puerto Rico with heavy concentrations of dinoflagellates, which emit a distinctive blue glow when disturbed.

The glowing marine organisms are nice, but for divers La Parguera is synonymous with wall diving. A tumultuous drop-off of continental proportion—like an underwater Grand Canyon—stretches more than 20 miles (32km) east and west

The mangrove lagoons near La Parguera act as nurseries for juvenile reef fish.

from Guánica. The reef reaches out from shore for about 7 miles (11km). The mostly flat reeftop plateau averages about 65ft (20m), but is etched with canyons that drop down about 15 to 20ft (4.5 to 6m). The first major drop falls away steeply to a broad shelf at 600ft (180m). From there, the canyon drops thousands more feet to join the oceanic depths of the Venezuelan Basin. A drop like this can be overwhelming. Divers should watch their depth gauges closely, explore only the top of the wall and stay within the sport-diving limit of 130ft (40m). Deeper areas remain a hidden arena known only to the creatures that inhabit the indigo world beyond. Visibility in the Parguera region is generally 60 to 100ft (18 to 30m).

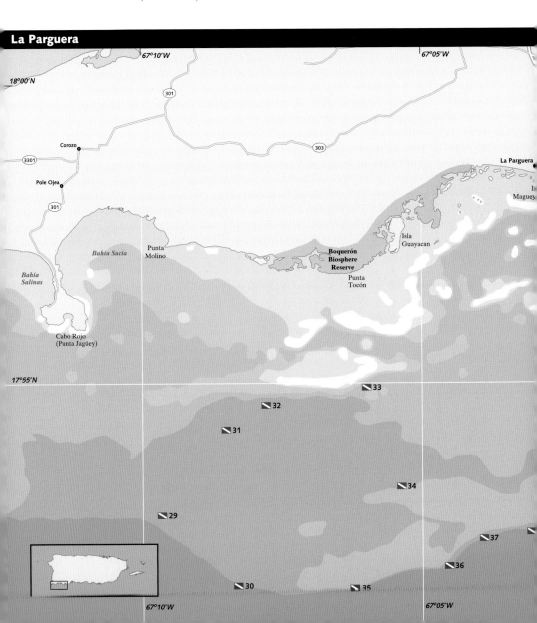

Deep Diving

Opportunities to dive deep abound in Puerto Rico, especially in the Parguera region off the south coast and around the western offshore islands of Desecheo and Mona. The temptation can be great to approach and surpass the recognized maximum sport-diving depth of 130ft (40m). Before venturing beyond this limit, it is imperative that divers be specially trained in deep diving and/or technical diving. Classes will teach you to recognize symptoms of nitrogen narcosis and to perform proper decompression procedures when doing deep or repetitive deep dives. Know your limits and don't push your luck when it comes to depth.

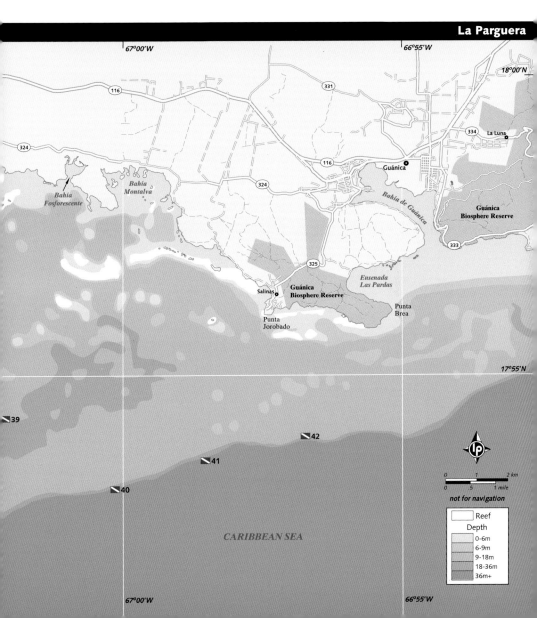

La Parguera

La Parguera Dive Sites

	Good Snorkeling	Novice	Intermediate	Advanced
29 Super Bowl			●	
30 The Chimney			●	
31 High Light			●	
32 The Motor		●		
33 Barracuda City		●		
34 The Star		●		
35 Hole in the Wall				●
36 Black Wall			●	
37 The Buoy			●	
38 Canyons		●		
39 1990		●		
40 Efra's Wall			●	
41 Two For You				●
42 Fallen Rock				●

29 Super Bowl

One of the area's westernmost dive sites, Super Bowl is a large basin scooped out of the reef plateau. Situated inshore of the drop-off, this site lies in 55 to 75ft and is usually dived as the shallower second dive of the day. The reef's many ledges create an undersea arena riddled with cavities, swim-throughs and overhangs. The reeftop itself is capped with stony brain corals, star corals and, most prevalently, boulder corals. Purple sea fans and tan sea rods provide a hiding place for trumpetfish.

Look for balloonfish or furry sea cucumbers in the sandy areas. Schools

Location: 5 miles (8km) south of Punta Molino

Depth Range: 55-75ft (17-23m)

Access: Boat

Expertise Rating: Intermediate

of deep-purple creole wrasse glide by, while large round French angelfish nibble away in tandem at the variety of sponges. Queen angelfish, the shyest of the angelfish species, play tag with each other. Their exquisite colors and fast movements make it difficult for photographers to capture their beauty on film.

If you have never seen the small, shy peppermint bass, this is the ideal hunting ground. Search dark recesses in the base of the reef for the fish's distinctive markings—bold stripes of maroon, pink and gold with light-blue highlights on the tips of the fins. Also look for the scrawled cowfish, which has a hard exoskeleton and sharp spines that stick up over its eyes and below its tail. The cowfish can change color quickly from blue-green to a yellowish brown. Expect to see pompano and bar jacks patrolling the outer areas.

30 The Chimney

The Chimney is a north-facing ledge honeycombed with holes. The ledge begins at 55ft and descends to 75ft. This dive is generally done as a second dive of the day. You'll descend to the anchor, swim a short distance to the drop-off, then descend to depth along the reef face. Midway through the dive, you'll see the chimney for which the site is named. Enter it from the bottom and swim up the beautifully sculpted chute, which leads you up to the reef peak at 55ft. From here, divers are encouraged to stay on top and slowly work their way back to the boat. Nearly all of the diving in the Parguera region is done in this type of rectangular multi-level pattern.

Location: 6.5 miles (10km) south of Punta Molino

Depth Range: 55-75ft (17-23m)

Access: Boat

Expertise Rating: Intermediate

tection for denizens such as the large green moray and smaller golden-brown chain moray. Trumpetfish drift at odd angles with the gently swaying sea rods and cactus corals. With a wave of excitement, schools of purple and orange creole wrasse wing in and out of sight, spilling over the reef like a magestic waterfall.

The sides of the ledge are sprayed purple with coralline algae. The reef crest is covered in a thin layer of pink calcified algae, an important reef-building element. Yellow-and-silver striped French grunts cluster together along the ledge. Torpedo-shaped bluehead wrasse swim quickly above the palette of hard corals on top. The reef's many holes give ample pro-

The Chimney presents striking photo opportunities.

31 High Light

The reef at High Light is carpeted with an artistically displayed assortment of corals and sponges. Visibility averages around 75ft and is frequently in excess of 100ft. The clear water makes it easy to catch a glimpse of fast-moving pelagics like cero mackerel or schools of ocean triggerfish.

Narrow canyons wind their way to the wall. The reef bursts with creatures including purple-tipped sea anemones and their resident Pederson cleaner shrimp. Clusters of smooth brown tube sponges form shapes like moose antlers. Tangled masses of pink and red rope sponges, often covered with winding chains of golden zooanthids, add lovely

Location: 4 miles (6.4km) southeast of Punta Molino

Depth Range: 65-100ft (20-30m)

Access: Boat

Expertise Rating: Intermediate

combinations of color. Tightly packed corals are found above 100ft. As at most of the wall sections in this region, divers may see an endless stream of dark-purple and orange creole wrasse winging through the water with their pectoral fins.

32 The Motor

Several miles out to sea, but closer to shore than the main drop-off, an air-plane motor and its propeller sit in the sand. The whereabouts of the rest of the aircraft remains a mystery.

The reef forms several underwater amphitheaters nearby. The sides of the reef are honeycombed with deep holes and cracks where divers might see spotted

Location: 4 miles (6.4km) southeast of Punta Molino

Depth Range: 55-75ft (17-23m)

Access: Boat

Expertise Rating: Novice

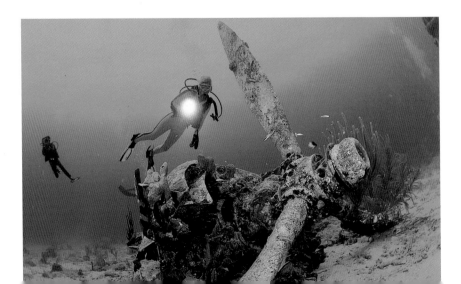

moray eels. Look for porkfish and schools of striped French grunts. In one place, two overhangs merge to form a box canyon. A hollow at the back of this canyon is wildly sprayed with encrusting sponges in every shade of red. Squirrelfish and blackbar soldierfish linger in this shaded spot.

Artificial Reefs

The best way for divers to understand reef evolution is to observe artificial reefs at different stages of development. An artificial reef can be established with almost any submerged foreign object—most often it will be a ship or plane wreck, but also "junk" like tires, bottles or even concrete blocks. The abundance of marine life and coral growth on an artificial reef depends on three main factors:

Location Natural and artificial reefs shelter animals from currents and from predators. Artificial reefs in open areas become an oasis for surrounding marine life. In current-swept locations, wrecks often attract species that are otherwise rare.

Material Steel provides an easy surface for coral to grow on, but rubber and aluminum objects are more difficult.

Age Generally, coral takes at least a few years to establish itself. The longer the object has been underwater, the more populated the artificial reef becomes.

33 Barracuda City

As the name implies, barracuda are common at this site, keeping a watchful eye over their watery domain. Barracuda City lies in shore of the reef's first big drop-off. Fingers of sand at about 70ft separate large spur-and-groove coral formations. Strong stands of elkhorn coral reach up toward the sunlight and are surrounded by assemblages of more-delicate staghorn coral. It is essential to maintain good buoyancy control to avoid damaging the immaculate coral arrangements.

Black durgon are abundant in this area, and you'll often catch rock beauties snacking on nests of sergeant major eggs. Lavender sea fans sway back and forth and, out in the sand, piles of coral debris house long, eel-like tilefish. Tiny blue chalk bass hover in small

Location: 5 miles (8km) southeast of La Parguera

Depth Range: 60-70ft (18-21m)

Access: Boat

Expertise Rating: Novice

Shy black durgon tend to retreat into small crevices.

groups over sandy areas—they can be approached and photographed if you use slow, nonthreatening movements. Look also for green morays—you might see a head poking out of one of the recesses along the reef. A close look may reveal the antennae of heavily armored spiny lobsters.

34 The Star

In this area, you'll find a convergence of irregular coral mounds perched on top of a sand plateau. Their sharp points come together to form a large starlike pattern in the sand. This convenient assemblage of coral hills lies in about 65ft, topping out at 45ft. If you're taking photos here, you'll find it easier to set up on the bottom near the reef base to best capture the vertical relief. This position lends itself to slight upward angles, allowing you to capture more light from the surface.

Large areas of sand next to the reefs offer a wide variety of marine life. You may be surprised to learn that a third or more of the fish you see during the day, including wrasse, actually bury themselves inches below the sand each night. Look for circular concave holes dug in the sandy channels surrounding the reefs—these show where southern stingrays have been feeding recently.

Location: 6.5 miles (10km) southeast of La Parguera

Depth Range: 45-65ft (14-20m)

Access: Boat

Expertise Rating: Novice

Look also for the nesting sites of sand tilefish. Tilefish gather finger-sized bits of coral debris and deposit them in a mound, leaving room inside for their protection. Light-blue or white, tilefish grow to about 2ft long and are commonly seen hovering a foot or more off the bottom. Tilefish tend to be shy and retreat quickly when approached.

At this site, there's no shortage of colorful sponges, soft corals and busy tropicals. You'll usually see barracuda, as well as the clusters of black durgon flip-flopping their fins in the warm, clear water.

35 Hole in the Wall

One of the deepest planned dives in the Parguera region, Hole in the Wall is great for advanced divers. You'll descend to 125ft and swim through a hole at the base of a short steep peninsula that reaches out from the wall. The main feature of the dive is the swim-through. Although there is plenty of good diving on top of the reef at 65ft, the best diving takes place along the wall, generally below 80ft, where you'll find impressive reef structure and relief.

Location: 9 miles (14km) southeast of La Parguera

Depth Range: 50-125ft (15-38m)

Access: Boat

Expertise Rating: Advanced

You'll have to gently push whip corals out of the way as you swim up through the hole. The hole offers underwater photographers a chance to capture stunning silhouettes. However, shooting at these depths can pose additional challenges even for skilled underwater photographers. Metering light, calculating distances, and aiming and adjusting lights can be difficult at depth.

36 Black Wall

To get to Black Wall, the boat departs from La Parguera and travels east on the peaceful water of the inner lagoon, then south through the low-lying islands. At this site, a large three-sided bowl is scooped out of the top of the wall, the sides of which drop hundreds of feet. Enormous red and black deepwater gorgonians mixed with bushy trees of black coral can be found all along the top and sides, extending down beyond 130ft.

Location: 8 miles (13km) south of La Parguera

Depth Range: 60-130ft (18-40m)

Access: Boat

Expertise Rating: Intermediate

This area is one of the steepest drop-offs along the wall. The current tends to be light to moderate, but the surface can be rough with 3 to 5ft waves.

These waters are home to many baboon-faced black durgons, which prefer the deepwater sites. These triggerfish swim in mid-water or just below the surface. Along the edge of the reef, large dog snappers, bright-blue queen angels and sinister-looking Spanish hogfish zoom in and out of seascapes filled with orange and red corals, lavender rope sponges and yellow and purple tube sponges.

The wall is alive with a pleasing array of colors. Underwater photographers will find little reason to leave the environment carved out of the wall. The rich, warm colors of the corals contrast nicely with the clear deep-blue background.

A diver examines a healthy stand of purple tube sponges.

37 The Buoy

Several miles southeast of La Parguera, within sight of the dry forest hills of Guánica, lies The Buoy. The site is named for a buoy that once served as a marker for scientific purposes. The buoy itself is long gone—all that remains is the large cement block it was once tied to. Healthy corals and invertebrate life stretch out in all directions. The entire area is remarkably intact and shows little, if any, evidence of storm damage.

The drop-off here is not as sheer as in some other spots. The wall starts at about 65ft and, though depths in excess of 100ft are easily reached, 80ft is a good average for divers, allowing plenty of time for exploring. Narrow canyons carved deep into the reef face lead to the wall, forming rivers of sand that cascade well out of sight. Giant red-brown barrel sponges

Location: 7 miles (11km) south of La Parguera

Depth Range: 65-100ft (20-30m)

Access: Boat

Expertise Rating: Intermediate

abound on the deep, sloping reef. Pink vase sponges crawling with brittlestars and azure vase sponges hold their color well, even at 100ft. Twenty-armed golden crinoids—members of the feather star class—hide their sticky appendages. Divers floating in the company of a wealth of reef fish will find it easy to cruise through four or five of these hard-coral canyons before returning to the boat.

The profuse sponge life along the Parguera wall makes an impressive backdrop for divers' videos.

38 Canyons

As the name implies, this site boasts steep-walled canyons cut through ancient reef formations of densely packed hard corals. At 65ft, the reeftop consists of a broad band of low-lying corals that runs parallel to the contours of the drop-off. The reeftop plateau is etched with canyons perpendicular to the wall every 50 to 75ft. These sunken canyons drop 15 to 20ft through layers of brain, boulder and sheet corals.

The canyons transport divers directly to the reef edge. You'll quickly descend to 85ft and swim through tall church-door openings to the wall, which slopes well out of sight. If you swim along the wall and maintain a depth of 85 to 100ft, you can experience three or four more of these canyons before turning back to the boat.

Inside the canyons, long purple tube sponges stick out in places, and orange icing sponges lace the undersides of the corals. Look for golden crinoids and even a large green moray. Great barracuda swim up above, along with groups of black durgons. These dark blue-green fish appear black from a

Location: 7 miles (11km) south of La Parguera

Depth Range: 65-110ft (20-34m)

Access: Boat

Expertise Rating: Novice

distance—note the fine light-blue or white line along the upper and lower fins.

Canyons is also blessed with an enormous school of more than 500 Atlantic spadefish. These shiny silver-and-black fish form a spiraling cloud that may encircle a diver or funnel down to visit an established cleaning station. The spadefish lie sideways on the coral, allowing the cleaner fish to devour parasites from their scales. Spadefish frequent Canyons regularly, so your chances of seeing this huge ball of fish up close are quite good. Unfortunately, the spadefish sometimes disappear for unexplained periods of as long as two months.

39 1990

Out of a flat sand bottom at 70ft rise rounded hills of mound and boulder corals splashed with brilliant orange, yellow and red rope sponges and large colonies of sea plumes and fans. Schools of little electric-blue chromis swim in mid-water above the reefs, and nearly a dozen varieties of wrasse swim dizzily around the seascape. Large French angelfish have adopted the curious habit of playfully nipping at the steady supply of

Location: 4 miles (6.4km) south of La Parguera

Depth Range: 55-70ft (17-21m)

Access: Boat

Expertise Rating: Novice

divers' bubbles. A large sandy area in the center of all the coral is a proven spot to spy southern stingrays concealed under, or swimming over, the sand.

40 Efra's Wall

Affectionately named for Efra Figuera, a local dive-shop owner, this is a moderate dive that takes place mainly between 80 and 100ft. It is an especially good spot for photographers because you'll find many different creatures including crabs, slipper lobsters and an abundance of golden, beaded and black-and-white crinoids.

Location: 6 miles (9.7km) southeast of La Parguera

Depth Range: 55-120ft (17-37m)

Access: Boat

Expertise Rating: Intermediate

The long thin wires of whip corals are so prolific here that you literally have to push them out of your way to pass through the deep canyons. In some places, the deepwater gorgonians growing out of opposing canyon walls are so dense that they create an impenetrable mesh of living coral.

Common here and throughout most of the Caribbean, golden zooanthids can be seen covering green finger sponges and thin rope sponges.

Efra's Wall is just one section of the drop-off stretching for 20 miles along the south coast.

41 Two For You

Two for You is one of a number of serious deep dives in this area. Here, two rock projections extend from the wall, separated by only a short swim. The reef begins at 55ft and the best depths for exploring the sheer drop are between 90 and 120ft.

The artistically arranged azure vase sponges and red rope sponges are laced with fingers of gorgonians and golden feather stars, making the reef look like an underwater flower shop. Each of the peninsulas hosts a heavy concentration of sponges and soft corals—they look like giant hands offering bouquets of coral and lace to some beautiful sea goddess.

Location: 6.5 miles (10km) southwest of Guánica

Depth Range: 55-120ft (17-37m)

Access: Boat

Expertise Rating: Advanced

Small peppermint bass hide around the deep ledges. Indigo hamlets, spotfin butterflyfish and silver jacks are among the many fish parading here and there. Currents along the wall are mild at most. The boat ride out can be rough but it's always calm underwater.

Clusters of smooth brown tube sponges form shapes like moose antlers.

42 Fallen Rock

This is one of the best dives along the entire wall that stretches from the lighthouse at Cabo Rojo to Guánica. Ages ago, at the site that is now known as Fallen Rock, a huge section of rock broke off and slid down the face of the wall, creating a V-shaped notch in the wall. Over the years, this rock slide has acted like a magnet attracting abundant corals and brilliant sponges, and a multitude of marine invertebrates have found sanctuary around this deep underwater pinnacle. The pinnacle exerts a similarly powerful attraction to divers from Guánica and La Parguera.

Location: 5 miles (8km) southwest of Guánica

Depth Range: 65-120ft (20-37m)

Access: Boat

Expertise Rating: Advanced

Just past the reef crest you'll see the vertical and undercut cliffs surrounding the site. A dramatic descent takes you to the outer base, where black coral trees grow everywhere. As you approach the sport-diving depth limit, a mildly intoxicating nitrogen narcosis will kick in, perhaps enhancing your experience of the bright-blue clusters of tiny chromis or the rich golds and blues of queen angelfish.

After a short time at the bottom, begin to spiral back up the rock past volcano sponges and ledges dripping with gorgonians. Back on the reeftop, cero mackerel cruise the wall and a school of Caesar grunts fills a narrow canyon. Long safety stops on the line are the norm at the end of the dive.

A dramatic descent makes Fallen Rock the area's finest dive.

Cabo Rojo Dive Sites

The west coast of Puerto Rico runs in an almost straight line for 35 miles (56km). The region's two main cities, Mayagüez in the south and Aguadilla in the north, have major airports that can accommodate large jets and direct flights from the United States. The smaller communities of Boquerón and Rincón best exemplify life along the west coast. The tranquil bays of sparkling clear water and palm-lined white-sand beaches offer a perfect place to hang your hammock.

Until recently, the coast south of Mayagüez, down to the lighthouse at Cabo Rojo, was largely overlooked by recreational divers. This area lies between two of the best dive regions in Puerto Rico—La Parguera and Desecheo—so it stands to reason that there should be some excellent diving. Diving here is only now being explored, but it is fair to say that the southwest offers a hybrid of the wall diving found in La Parguera and the super-rich reefs surrounding Desecheo. Also, the surface waters are much calmer than at dive regions to the north and east. In the shallow areas, you'll find patch reefs crisscrossed with tiny sand corridors. The deeper waters hold well-established coral formations with steep walls, overhangs and undercut ledges. You are unlikely to see other boats while diving this area.

Diving conditions on the west coast are ideal year-round. The nearshore waters are kept in the lee from the prevailing trade winds nearly all year, which means that seas are flat and waters tend to be clear. Ongoing scouting of the reefs and drop-offs in this area is quickly putting this region of Puerto Rico on the diving map.

The rugged Cabo Rojo coast is a new divers' playground.

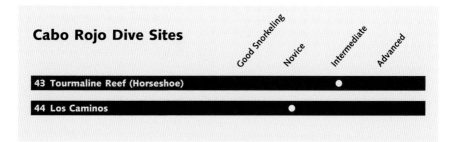

Cabo Rojo Dive Sites	Good Snorkeling	Novice	Intermediate	Advanced
43 Tourmaline Reef (Horseshoe)			●	
44 Los Caminos		●		

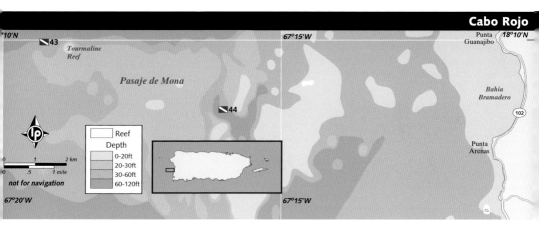

Cabo Rojo

	Reef
	Depth
	0-20ft
	20-30ft
	30-60ft
	60-120ft

not for navigation

43 Tourmaline Reef (Horseshoe)

Thanks to the true spirit of adventure, new dive areas are continually being chartered around Cabo Rojo and Maya-güez. Tourmaline Reef is one of these new areas. Fishermen have known of this expansive reef area for decades, but it was only recently that divers began to take notice. At this site, also sometimes called Horseshoe, the bottom is a bit silty, reducing visibility to about 50ft.

The reeftop begins at about 40ft and sharply cuts back on itself while slicing down to 90ft. Tourmaline is a perfect 90ft dive—all the best stuff is near the bottom and along the steep sides of the drop-off. The most interesting part of the dive is the shape and size of bot-

Location: 11 miles (18km) west of Punta Guanajibo

Depth Range: 40-90ft (12-27m)

Access: Boat

Expertise Rating: Intermediate

tom contours, which offer building-size boulders, deep undercuts and overhangs. Currents run moderate to strong. Once down you can always find protection from the current between large valleys of soft sand. The bottom is silty, so avoid kicking up the sediments.

The reef is alive with huge bushy trees of black coral, sea whips and healthy gorgonians. There are large orange deepwater fans and schools of shimmering grunts and bright goatfish. For the underwater photographer, Tourmaline Reef offers a wealth of dramatic wide-angle opportunities, as well as dozens of creatures for close-up macro work.

This area is a short 20-minute ride from Joyuda, less if departing from Mayagüez. When seas are running big, this is a great alternative to the longer trip and rougher seas near Desecheo. In time even more areas nearby will be discovered, opening up an even larger chapter in diving Puerto Rico's west side.

Divers have only recently begun to explore the diving possibilities of the area's healthy reefs.

44 Los Caminos

At Los Caminos, a pleasant and relatively shallow series of canals spreads out over the seafloor. The terrain doesn't offer a great deal of relief, but what the area lacks in dramatic scale, it more than makes up for in marine life.

Look for rosy and pearly razorfish out in the sunny sand channels. Razorfish cultivate loose holes of sand, which they dive into to escape predators. The holes

Location: 5 miles (8km) west of Punta Arenas

Depth Range: 30-40ft (9-12m)

Access: Boat

Expertise Rating: Novice

are tough to spot, but look for a razorfish hovering head down just in front of one. Tiny mollusks, such as flamingo tongues, purple-spotted sea goddesses and long-horn nudibranchs, flourish in the nutrient-rich waters. Blue tangs, surgeonfish and doctorfish hold mobile conventions in shades of blue. Bright, sticky-fingered crinoids fill crevices, while tiny peppermint gobies lie perched on star corals. Aquamarine Y-branching algae and spindly arrow crabs dot the reefscape, along with a wonderful variety of painted tunicates, bluebell tunicates and giant tunicates.

Tunicates: Spineless Chordates

One of the Caribbean's most common marine invertebrates, tunicates are often mistaken for sponges. Like the sponge, they usually have two siphons, one for drawing in nutrients and the other for expelling used water. Though some are free-swimming, most tunicates are attached to the reef at one end and come in a variety of often-brilliant colors. Sometimes the tunicate is covered in algal growth, making it difficult to spot unless it is feeding and its siphon is open.

These creatures are difficult to photograph because they are light and pressure sensitive—when disturbed, muscular bands around the siphons rapidly contract. The common name "tunicate" comes from the animal's cellulose body covering or "tunic." They are also commonly called "sea squirts" because some species, when irritated, will forcefully expel a stream of water from their excurrent opening. Tunicates may live singularly or in a colony, and sometimes a number of compound tunicates live together inside a common tunic with multiple incurrent siphons and a larger excurrent siphon.

Perhaps most unique about the tunicate is its seemingly unusual classification. Normally, chordates have backbones and are vertebrates. Not so with the tunicate. Classified as a urochordate, the tunicate has no backbone, but is still included in the Chordata phylum. Why? At some point in the life cycle, all urochordates have a tail, a dorsal central nerve cord, pharyngael gill clefts and, at the larval stage, a notochord, which is a flexible, supportive rod made of cartilage. In vertebrates, the notochord is replaced by bone.

Northwest Dive Sites

Puerto Rico's northwest corner is considered the island's beach-diving capital. Popular north- and west-facing beaches around the towns of Isabela and Aguadilla can be dived most of the year. Winter swells in the north create excellent surfing conditions at Jobos (pronounced HO-bos) Beach and south of Aguadilla at Rincón. The surf conditions often dictate the best time and place for beach diving.

The nutrient-rich waters off the northwest coast abound with marine life. The ultra-healthy reef environment fosters incredible smaller critters like nudibranchs, Christmas tree worms, rough fileclams and sponge zooanthids. Sharpnose puffers are everywhere and scorpionfish are another common sight.

A beached fishing boat in Rincón.

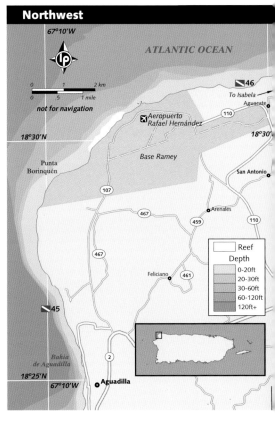

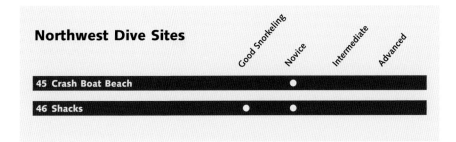

Northwest Dive Sites

	Good Snorkeling	Novice	Intermediate	Advanced
45 Crash Boat Beach			●	
46 Shacks		●	●	

45 Crash Boat Beach

This is the most popular beach dive in all of Puerto Rico and is a popular spot for conducting Open Water training dives at all levels. The story goes that the beach earned its unusual name because some 50 years ago the military practiced beach landings here. Local fishermen continue the tradition with their unique way of beaching their flat-bottomed wooden boats—upon returning from a morning fishing trip, they launch their boats full blast toward the beach, hurling them clear of the water.

Traveling north or south through Agua-dilla on Route 111, look for the large Crash Boat highway sign. Turn west at the big church and follow a narrow and winding road to a municipal park with palm trees, picnic tables, a pier and a boardwalk with ven-dors. The beach is lined with colorfully painted fishing boats with their pointed bows angled up in the air.

Location: West of Aguadilla's beach

Depth Range: 0-60ft (0-18m)

Access: Shore

Expertise Rating: Novice

Entry is easy if you head to the right of the pier, away from boat traffic. Use the pier's pilings to navigate down to 30ft.

Though visibility varies, divers are rewarded with plenty of marine life.

Underwater, look for giant barrel sponges and bright yellow patches of encrusting social tunicates. Follow the pier underwater to the end and then turn right. You'll see all sorts of debris, and the rows of pilings make interesting silhouettes. Crash Boat Beach is a good critter dive, with huge scorpionfish, lots of fireworms, striped and longsnout butterflyfish, and

literally dozens of sharpnose pufferfish. Blackbar soldierfish frequent the area, and it is a promising spot to see both yellow and red longlure frogfish.

With visibility of 50ft and better, the water is relatively clear for a beach dive. There is a lot of monofilament fishing line present at this location, so it's a good idea to carry a knife.

46 Shacks

Named for some wooden shacks on top of a rocky peninsula, this shallow beach dive and snorkeling spot is best done with one of the dive operators from Aguadilla or Isabela. Though this is not a difficult dive, it's best to go with a guide familiar with the lay of the land. Knowledgeable guides conduct beach dives daily and have flexible schedules that cater to small groups. If you are not staying at nearby Villa Tropical or Villa Montaña, ask first about gaining access to Shacks Beach through their property. Dive companies have access pre-cleared.

Entering the water, you'll have to negotiate several shallow sandstone

Location: North of Isabela's beach

Depth Range: 5-30ft (1.5-9m)

Access: Shore

Expertise Rating: Novice

ledges before reaching water deep enough to swim in. The summer months (May to November) are best for diving Shacks, and the calmest conditions occur at low tide, when the waves are broken up by the outer reef. The dive site itself isn't far offshore—after entering, you'll swim through openings in the reef. Your guide will lead you through a maze of caverns and canyons, but you'll rarely dip below 30ft. The lighting is moody and spectacular and each cave entrance is different from the next one.

Manatees occasionally visit this area. Look also for plenty of sheet corals, carpet anemones and schools of goatfish, grunts and blue tangs. A number of different underwater routes lead you back to the spot where you began your dive. The mysterious maze of grottos makes it easy to see why hiring a guide makes for a much

Carpet anemones cover large areas.

more enjoyable experience.

Isla Desecheo Dive Sites

The island of Desecheo lies about 14 miles (23km) west of the Puerto Rican mainland surfing community of Rincón. Surrounded by tremendously deep waters that support a super-charged reef environment and boast visibility better than 80ft (24m), Desecheo is possibly the best small island in the Caribbean to enjoy unspoiled diving.

Desecheo is a steep, rocky island covered with tropical dry forest. Large gumbo-limbo trees—characterized by their brown, brightly lacquered trunks—are common in the interior valleys, and a variety of cactus species make up the thorny scrub vegetation on the steep coastal slopes. Because of unexploded military ordnance, visitors are prohibited from going on land. Anchoring while diving or bird-watching is unregulated.

Small six-person boats make the 40-minute trip through the open seas from Rincón, sometimes encountering pilot whales, humpback whales and playful spinner dolphins on the way. The bottom contours along the journey are impressive—the sea between Rincón and Desecheo drops to 1,800ft (550m). As you approach Desecheo from the east, the bottom shelves back up to 300ft (90m) about a mile from the island.

In the waters around Desecheo, mountains of rock are transformed into a living tapestry of color crawling with marine creatures large and small. Away from the spectacular reefs, buoyed by billions of gallons of seawater, giant

Uninhabited Isla Desecheo is surrounded by some of Puerto Rico's best dive sites.

humpback whales emit lonely songs into the deep silent waters. The entire island is registered as a wildlife reserve, and plans are underway to establish a natural marine reserve for the coral reefs surrounding the 360-acre (145-hectare) island.

Diving Isla Mona

Fifty miles (80km) west of Mayagüez lies rugged Mona Island. Situated between Puerto Rico and the Dominican Republic in the rough waters of the Mona Passage, Mona is sometimes considered the Galápagos of the Caribbean because of its remote natural beauty. Seabirds nest on Mona nearly every month of the year. Species include brown- and red-footed boobies as well as red-billed and white-tailed tropic birds. Green iguanas reside in the trees, while sturdier ground iguanas seek refuge in the abundant caves. The reefs surrounding the island offer excellent diving with clear water, magnificent scenery and lots of large fish like groupers, snappers and moray eels. Turtles, sharks, whales and dolphins are more common here than in most places in the Caribbean.

Mona is maintained as a nature refuge, so permits must be obtained from the Department of Natural and Environmental Resources before visits can be made. Dive operators plan special trips, usually once a month on weekends. Since the island has no facilities, diving and camping trips to Mona require lots of advance planning and a true appreciation for roughing it. At present, your best bet for getting to Mona is to contact Taíno Divers in Rincón, Paradise Scuba Center in La Parguera or the Boquerón Dive Shop in Boquerón. Paradise Scuba Center and Boquerón Dive Shop are owned and operated by the same family. Daytrips from Boquerón leave before dawn and return after dark, allowing enough time for two or sometimes three dives. Overnight camping trips (equipment and permits included) depart from Rincón, allowing for five dives.

As great as the stories are about Mona, you need to realize that it is a big trip. The crossing can take many hours, depending on the conditions. As you leave the Puerto Rican mainland behind, you enter the rough waters of the Mona Passage. The boats do fine, but your stomach and nerves may be another matter altogether. Even well-traveled sailors bringing their vessels south for the winter dread the infamous waterway. They prepare themselves and their vessels as best they can and then just hang on for as many hours as it takes until they once again enter calmer waters. If you happen upon a calm-weather period during your trip, you should consider yourself very lucky.

Not many divers in the world will ever get to experience this legendary Caribbean island. Trips are often cancelled at the last minute for bad weather or sudden schedule changes. Conservation-minded divers should be aware that plenty of hunting takes place here. Once you arrive at Mona (or nearby Monita), many divers jump into the clear waters armed with spearguns, pole spears, lobster snares and anything else that they can use to kill their prey. Mona's waters boast big fish, lots of turtles and plenty of sharks, along with huge drop-offs and deep and unimaginably clear water.

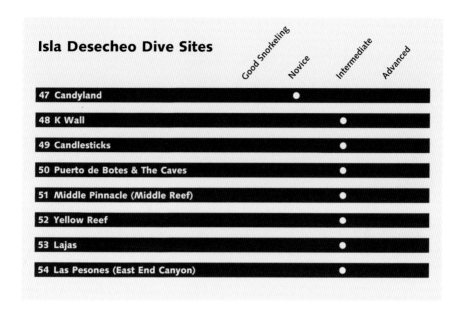

Isla Desecheo Dive Sites

	Good Snorkeling	Novice	Intermediate	Advanced
47 Candyland		●		
48 K Wall			●	
49 Candlesticks			●	
50 Puerto de Botes & The Caves			●	
51 Middle Pinnacle (Middle Reef)			●	
52 Yellow Reef			●	
53 Lajas			●	
54 Las Pesones (East End Canyon)			●	

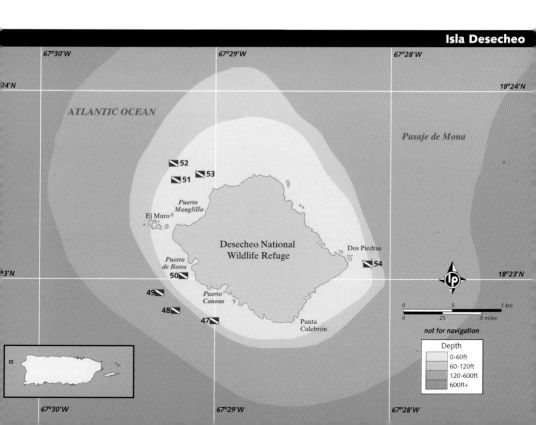

Isla Desecheo

ATLANTIC OCEAN

Pasaje de Mona

52
51 53

Puerto Manglillo
El Muro

Desecheo National
Wildlife Refuge

Dos Piedras

Puerto de Botes
50 54

49
Puerto Canoas
48
47

Punta Culebrón

not for navigation

Depth	
	0-60ft
	60-120ft
	120-600ft
	600ft+

0 .5 1 km
0 .25 .5 miles

67°30'W 67°29'W 67°28'W
18°24'N
18°23'N

47 Candyland

Location: Southwest side of Desecheo

Depth Range: 60-80ft (18-24m)

Access: Boat

Expertise Rating: Novice

While there are excellent dives all around Desecheo, the southwest sites farthest away from the mainland are favored by some divers for their calmer surface conditions. Here, large patch reefs are separated by sand flats. The corals extend in all directions, and the relief from the sand to the top of the coral heads is about 20ft.

The reef in this area is extra healthy, with impressive castle-shaped boulder corals, 6ft-tall sea fans, flower-coral colonies, endlessly sprawling sheet and lettuce corals and plenty of fantastically colorful sponges. Look for dense schools of yellow-and-white goatfish, pairs of reef butterflyfish and rock beauties in every phase of development. Several uncommon fish species can also be observed, such as the web burrfish and conies in their golden phase.

48 K Wall

Location: Southwest side of Desecheo

Depth Range: 60-100ft (18-30m)

Access: Boat

Expertise Rating: Intermediate

The reefs on the leeward side of Desecheo foster well-groomed marine gardens populated by enormous sea fans and healthy beds of coral. K Wall is somewhat misnamed—rather than a wall, you'll find broad shelves of layered hard corals cascading from a gently sloping sand bottom. The shelves start in about 75ft and

Colorful sponges and reef fish thrive in the marine gardens at K Wall.

continue away from shore, reaching depths in excess of 100ft. The coral shelves are shaped vaguely like continents—explore the artful blend of coral summits and saucer-coral plains of each "country." The remaining spaces are packed with large orange elephant ear sponges, and long red rope sponges stand tall in the protected waters.

The surge can be heavy when a north or west swell is present. Visibility typically exceeds 100ft, allowing you great views of gigantic sea turtles floating by in the deep. In the shallows, watch the groups of fish mingling in formations above the reef. You might see schools of shiny gray chubs mixed with pale ocean triggerfish and the occasional group of quick creole wrasse fling by. Sticking close to the protection afforded by coral cover, bright-yellow and jet-black rock beauties turn on a dime.

49 Candlesticks

This dive is good from the bottom up. Candlesticks is a lovely patch reef interspersed with several channels. The unbelievable color and clarity of the water in this area allows you to make out the forms and textures of corals as far as 80ft below you. The boulder corals here look like thick piles of melted candle wax, the undersides of which are laced with bright yellow-orange icing sponges.

Location: 50 yards (45m) west of Desecheo

Depth Range: 60-90ft (18-27m)

Access: Boat

Expertise Rating: Intermediate

from the island and you can easily find yourself at 90ft.

Sparkling blue chromis seem to be suspended over each coral mountain. This, together with a bramble of row pore rope sponges, stony flower corals and assorted tropical reef fish, show the cornucopia of brilliant marine life at this site. Pay close attention to your depth gauge because the reef gradually slopes as you head away

The boulder corals at Candlesticks look like melted wax.

50 Puerto de Botes & The Caves

The peninsula of large rocks around Desecheo's northwest point acts as a barrier protecting the shallows from the open ocean swells to the north. Inside this cover, the shoreline is riddled with rock caves and a crescent-shaped pebble beach. Visibility is excellent in these waters, but currents sometimes kick up.

Location: West of Desecheo

Depth Range: 10-80ft (3-24m)

Access: Boat

Expertise Rating: Intermediate

The ocean is bountiful in this area. If you're lucky, the boat ride to and from this site might reveal a pod of spinner dolphins leaping and tumbling clear of the water. The dive site encompasses two different diving environments, one deep and one shallow, which have two different names. Divers usually begin in Puerto de Botes, the deeper part farther from shore. This area boasts hard-coral foothills separated by bright sand valleys, all in about 60 to 80ft. From there, divers swim toward the rocky shoreline, arriving at the shallow area called The Caves. The steep-walled stone canyons nearest shore are predominantly one color—red. The corallite colonies along the shallow walls and cave ceilings are overgrown with sponges, algae and other encrusting organisms. The colors in the rest of the site range from incredible red-oranges to purples. Schools of tropical fish hang suspended above the coral contours, while nurse sharks rest in any of a variety of choice sheltered spots.

It is difficult to find a spot around Desecheo that is not dripping with brilliant color.

51 Middle Pinnacle (Middle Reef)

On the northwest side of Desecheo, a series of rocky pinnacles runs in a straight line out from a rugged cove. The outer rise, less than a mile offshore, is **Yellow Reef** (Dive Site #52). Inside the confines of the cove, closest to the shore, is a shallow rise. Situated between the two, a few hundred yards offshore, is the Middle Pinnacle dive site, also called Middle Reef.

Location: Northwest side of Desecheo

Depth Range: 30-65ft (9-20m)

Access: Boat

Expertise Rating: Intermediate

Often done as a second dive because of its moderate depths, Middle Pinnacle is essentially a cluster of lava rocks riddled with a labyrinth of grottos. Corridors run out from a central rock in every direction like a spoked wagon wheel. These swim-throughs come in all sizes and effectively double the surface area that corals and other invertebrates can attach to. Middle Pinnacle encompasses too many areas to explore completely on a single dive.

Each grotto, large or small, is smothered in yellow, orange and red sponges highlighted by branching rose lace corals. Look directly beneath the spot where the boat anchors for a perfect rock arch that spans a canyon littered with tiny sponges.

The most common fish inhabitant is the coney. The coney is a relatively small sea bass that exhibits three distinctive color phases. Most often, the coney is brown with a red-circled eye and covered

Middle Reef is riddled with arches and corridors of all sizes.

with small blue dots. In its bicolor phase, the coney is dark brown or red on top and white below, with the blue spots still present. The least common phase is the most striking—the entire fish is a brilliant yellow-gold, with only a smattering of blue spots. Divers occasionally see the coney in its rare golden phase in this area.

52 Yellow Reef

The classical myth of Poseidon, the Greek god of the ocean, has him and his beautiful wife Amphitrite living in a golden palace beneath the sea. Standing alone north of Desecheo and closest to the colossal depths of the Puerto Rican Trench, Yellow Reef could be this palace. Here, a mighty mountain decorated with an almost supernatural profusion of yellow, orange and golden sponges juts up from the seafloor.

As seen from the surface, a straight line of dark blue water marks where the face of this sculpted rock wall drops down,

Location: Northwest of Desecheo

Depth Range: 25-100+ft (7.5-30+m)

Access: Boat

Expertise Rating: Intermediate

beginning with a sharp undercut. The dive begins at 30ft, where the unhesitatingly vertical wall leads down to 70ft. There, the rock reef splits in all directions, forming large caves at 90 to 100ft.

Giant anemones can move in a snail-like manner, but generally stay put.

Current-driven nutrients bathe the magnificent seascape—the diversity of marine life is so rich that one simply cannot find an area not dripping with color. For photographers, a single dive or a single roll of film will not be sufficient. Yellow Reef offers many other marine wonders, from tiny spinyhead blennies darting out of wormholes to grab suspended particles of food, to humpback whales on their seasonal migrations north (January to March). The sizable fish population at this site includes tiger groupers, princess parrotfish, sargassum triggerfish and animated redlip blennies.

Yellow Reef is arguably the best dive in all of Puerto Rico. This high-ranking profile does come at a price, however— it is impossible to determine when the site will be plagued by exceptionally strong currents and heavy surge, rendering it off-limits for diving.

Underwater Photo Tips

Before departing for a dive site, have your camera completely set up and check that batteries and flash connections are good by test-firing the unit. Bring extra film or cameras and be ready for anything. Once onboard, be sure to store your cameras in a safe place away from heavy scuba equipment and out of direct sunlight. If possible, bring fresh water in a small cooler or bucket to soak and clean the camera immediately after your dive. Many dive operators understand the special needs of photographers, so take advantage of their knowledge and ask them to help you determine the best lens or subjects before each dive.

Once underwater, search, don't swim. Chasing fish only yields a bunch of poor tail shots. Approach subjects slowly using nonthreatening movements and minimize eye contact. You should get as close as possible to your subject and try to include some blue water in the background by angling upwards. Check and double-check that controls are set properly. Bracket your shots using different distance, f-stop or flash settings. For more impressive shots, fill the frame corner to corner.

Wide-angle lenses are best suited for reef scenes, diver portraits or silhouettes, caves, tunnels and shipwrecks. Fish portraits are more easily captured using longer lenses such as a 60mm or 105mm on cameras in housings or a 28mm or 35mm lens for Nikonos.

Close-ups or macros are ideal for night dives or when visibility is poor. They generally produce sharp, colorful images. Avoid trying to capture small fish with this set-up, however, because the framers tend to scare them away.

Photos of divers handling marine life are quickly becoming a thing of the past and are highly frowned upon by anyone concerned with conservation and safety. Remember: no photo is worth harming even the tiniest marine organism.

53 Lajas

On Desecheo's northwest side, Lajas is an ideal second dive of the day. It is similar to Yellow Reef, though smaller and easier to navigate. The underwater environment consists of short towers, arches, canyons and crevices. Explore the circumference of subsurface rocks and mountains blanketed with yellow and gold encrusting sponges.

Location: Northwest side of Desecheo

Depth Range: 30-70ft (9-21m)

Access: Boat

Expertise Rating: Intermediate

Along the base of the rocks, green-tipped giant sea anemones harbor squat anemone and cleaner shrimp. Look also for small banded clinging crabs peeking out from underneath the host's tentacles. Territorial bicolor damselfish patrol the reeftops, chasing off other small fish. A surplus of brilliant blue flecks gives away the position of dozens of juvenile blue chromis, while an equal number of their less-flashy brethren, the brown chromis, go practically unnoticed. Coarsely textured barrel sponges thrive here, and you'll see purple patches of an algae called reef cement just about anywhere that isn't already bursting with sponges or delicate branching corals. Currents and surge in this area can be strong.

54 Las Pesones (East End Canyon)

On the east side of Desecheo, closest to the Puerto Rican mainland, two triangular rocks break the surface. These rocks mark the site of a large undersea canyon, sometimes called East End Canyon. While most of the diving around Desecheo is on the protected west side, Las Pesones exemplifies the dramatic and rugged undersea terrain to the east. Conditions at this site can be a challenge—there is little protection from rough wind and waves, and currents and surges can be moderate to strong.

Location: Eastern point of Desecheo

Depth Range: 60-90ft (18-27m)

Access: Boat

Expertise Rating: Intermediate

Once inside the high-walled canyon, however, divers escape much of the currents above. The canyon walls deliver lots of vertical relief, forming what seems to be a box canyon. The canyon's underwater ridges lie in about 60ft, but the walls rapidly descend to 85ft and deeper in some spots. Small rock archways are fun to navigate, and the entire terrain is carpeted with layers of sponges accented by pretty pink and purple rose corals. Though void of large soft corals, the area is spray painted with yellow, orange and red sponges. Giant purple-tipped anemones nestled into the rock take advantage of the nutrients brought in by the tide. Large queen angelfish, rock beauties and barracuda also help to keep things interesting.

Delicate pink fans called rose corals abound on the reefs around Desecheo.

Marine Life

The creatures pictured here are just a sampling of the marine life that can be found in the waters that surround Puerto Rico. The island's mangrove estuaries and coral reefs are nurseries and feeding grounds for hundreds of Caribbean fish and invertebrate species. Puerto Rico is home to a particularly astounding array of sponges in many shapes, sizes and colors. Several species of endangered giant sea turtles nest on Puerto Rican beaches, especially in Culebra, while manatees (also endangered) cavort in mangrove estuaries along the south shore. Divers headed to Desecheo Island in the winter may glimpse or hear pilot and humpback whales.

Common names are used freely but are notoriously inaccurate and inconsistent. The two-part scientific name, usually shown in italics, is more precise. It consists of a genus name followed by a species name. A genus is a group of closely related species that share common features. A species is a recognizable group within a genus whose members are capable of interbreeding.

Common Vertebrates

gray angelfish
Pomacanthus arcuatus

queen angelfish
Holocanthus ciliaris

fairy basslet
Gramma loreto

diamond blenny
Malacoctenus boehlkei

redlip blenny
Ophioblennius atlanticus

black durgon
Melichthys niger

STEVE ROSENBERG

108

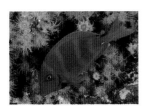

blue tang
Acanthurus coeruleus

banded butterflyfish
Chaetodon striatus

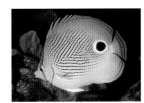

foureye butterflyfish
Chaetodon capistratus

reef butterflyfish
Chaetodon sedentarius

blue chromis
Chromis cyanea

spotted drum
Equetus punctatus

yellow goatfish
Mulloidichthys martinicus

sharknose goby
Gobiosoma evelynae

French grunt
Haemulon flavolineatum

barred hamlet
Hypoplectrus puella

hogfish
Lachnolaimus maximus

bar jack
Caranx ruber

yellowhead jawfish
Opistognathus aurifrons

stoplight parrotfish
Sparisoma viride

blackbar soldierfish
Myripristis jacobus

Atlantic spadefish
Chaetodipterus faber

bluehead wrasse
Thalassoma bifasciatum

creole wrasse
Clepticus parrae

Common Invertebrates

giant anemone
Condylactis gigantea

queen conch
Strombus gigas

yellowline arrow crab
Stenorhynchus seticornis

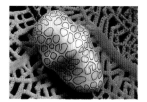

flamingo tongue
Cyphoma gibbosum

Caribbean spiny lobster
Panulirus argus

lettuce sea slug
Tridachia crispata

banded coral shrimp
Stenopus hispidus

Pederson cleaner shrimp
Periclimenes pedersoni

azure vase sponge
Callyspongia plicifera

STEVE ROSENBERG

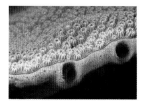

orange icing sponge
Mycale laevis

yellow tube sponge
Aplysina fistularis

blue bell tunicate
Clavelina puerto-secensis

Hazardous Marine Life

Marine animals almost never attack divers, but many have defensive and offensive weaponry that can be triggered if they feel threatened or annoyed. The ability to recognize hazardous creatures is a valuable asset in avoiding accident and injury. The following are some of the potentially hazardous creatures most commonly found in Puerto Rico.

Bristle Worm

Also called fire worms, bristle worms can be found on most reefs. They have segmented bodies covered with either tufts or bundles of sensory hairs that extend in tiny, sharp, detachable bristles. If you touch one, the tiny stinging bristles lodge in your skin and cause a burning sensation that may be followed by a red spot or welt. Remove embedded bristles with adhesive tape, rubber cement or a commercial facial peel. Apply a decontaminant such as vinegar, rubbing alcohol or dilute ammonia.

Fire Coral

Although often mistaken for stony coral, fire coral is a hydroid colony that secretes a hard, calcareous skeleton. Fire coral grows in many different shapes, often encrusting or taking the form of a variety of reef structures. It is usually identifiable by its tan, mustard or brown color and finger-like columns with whitish tips. The entire colony is covered by tiny pores and fine, hairlike projections nearly invisible to the unaided eye. Fire coral "stings" by discharging small, specialized cells called nematocysts. Contact causes a burning sensation that lasts for several minutes and may produce red welts on the skin. Do not rub the area, as you will only spread the stinging particles. Cortisone cream can reduce the inflammation and antihistamine cream is good for killing the pain. Serious stings should be treated by a doctor.

Stinging Hydroid

Contact with stinging hydroids may cause various degrees of skin irritation and several are toxic. Hydroids that sting include the stinging, branching, feather and bush species. Look for hydroids that are bushy and resemble plants with fernlike or feathery branches. Hydroids range in color from black or brown to gray or nearly white. The sting delivered is similar to that of fire coral, jellyfish or anemones. To treat the sting, flush the area with vinegar to neutralize the toxin and apply topical anesthetics, analgesics or ice packs to alleviate pain, swelling and irritation. Seek medical attention immediately for severe allergic reactions.

Jellyfish

Jellyfish sting by releasing the stinging cells contained in their trailing tentacles. As a rule, the longer the tentacles, the more painful the sting. Stings are often irritating and not painful, but should be treated immediately with a decontaminant such as vinegar, rubbing alcohol, baking soda, papain, or dilute household ammonia. Beware that some people may have a stronger reaction than others, in which case you should prepare to resuscitate and seek medical aid.

Moray Eel

Distinguished by their long, thick, snakelike bodies and tapered heads, moray eels come in a variety of colors and patterns. Don't feed them or put your hand in a dark hole—eels have the unfortunate combination of sharp teeth and poor eyesight, and will bite if they feel threatened. If you are bitten, don't try to pull your hand away suddenly—the teeth slant backward and are extraordinarily sharp. Let the eel release it and then surface slowly. Treat with antiseptics, anti-tetanus and antibiotics.

Scorpionfish

Scorpionfish are well-camouflaged creatures that have poisonous spines along their dorsal fins. They are often difficult to spot since they typically rest quietly on the bottom or on coral, looking more like rocks. Practice good buoyancy control and watch where you put your hands. Scorpionfish wounds can be excruciating. To treat a puncture, wash the wound and immerse in nonscalding hot water for 30 to 90 minutes. Administer pain medications if necessary.

STEVE ROSENBERG

Sea Urchin

Sea urchins tend to live in shallow areas near shore and come out of their shelters at night. They vary in coloration and size, with spines ranging from short and blunt to long and needle-sharp. The spines are the urchin's most dangerous weapon, easily able to penetrate neoprene wetsuits, booties and gloves. Treat minor punctures by extracting the spines and immersing in non-scalding hot water. More serious injuries require medical attention.

Shark

Sharks come in many shapes and sizes. They are most easily identified by their triangular dorsal fin. Though many species are shy, there are occasional attacks. About 25 species worldwide are considered dangerous to humans. Sharks will generally not attack unless provoked, so don't taunt, tease or feed them. Avoid spearfishing, carrying fish baits or mimicking a wounded fish and your likelihood of being attacked will greatly diminish. Face and quietly watch any shark that is acting aggressively and be prepared to push it away with camera, knife or tank. If someone is bitten by a shark, stop the bleeding, reassure the patient, treat for shock and seek immediate medical aid.

Fire Sponge

They may be beautiful, but sponges can pack a powerful punch with fine spicules that sting on contact, even after they've washed up on shore. Red sponges often carry the most potent sting, although they are not the only culprits. If you touch a stinging sponge, do not rub the area. Remove visible spicules with tweezers, adhesive tape, rubber cement or a commercial facial peel. Soak in vinegar for 10 to 15 minutes. The pain usually goes away within a day. Cortisone cream can help.

Diving Conservation & Awareness

Puerto Rico has long suffered from a number of serious environmental problems, including population growth and rapid urbanization, deforestation, erosion of soil, water pollution and mangrove destruction. While Puerto Ricans still have a long way to go toward undoing generations of environmental damage and preserving their natural resources, the past few decades have seen increased awareness, resources and action dedicated to conservation efforts.

Marine conservationists won several significant battles in the 1990s. In 1997, Isla Mona was declared a marine protection zone, and in August 1999, the Luis Peña Reef Natural Reserve was signed into existence. This 2.3 sq mile (3.7 sq km) no-take zone is situated off southeast Puerto Rico, between Culebra and Luis Peña Cay. Though modest in size, the reserve is rich in reef inhabitants and seagrass meadows known to be important nursery grounds for many reef fish. This reserve is a very big jump forward and will hopefully open the way for more no-take zones in Puerto Rico. Conservationists are trying to establish another no-take zone in the reef-rich marine area around Isla Desecheo.

Throughout Puerto Rico, individual dive operators are emerging as the new conservationists, acting as stewards and ambassadors of the reefs. Great efforts are being made to bring diving and fishing interests together in a cohesive plan that will allow the continuation of fishing while establishing much-needed no-take zones.

Responsible Diving

Dive sites tend to be located where the reefs and walls display the most beautiful corals and sponges. It only takes a moment—an inadvertently placed hand or knee, or a careless brush or kick with a fin—to destroy this fragile, living part of our delicate ecosystem. By following certain basic guidelines while diving, you can help preserve the ecology and beauty of the reefs:

1. Never drop boat anchors onto a coral reef and take care not to ground boats on coral. Encourage dive operators and regulatory bodies in their efforts to establish permanent moorings at appropriate dive sites.

2. Practice and maintain proper buoyancy control and avoid over-weighting. Be aware that buoyancy can change over the period of an extended trip. Initially you may breathe harder and need more weighting; a few days later you may breathe more easily and need less weight. Tip: Use your weight belt and tank position to maintain a horizontal position–raise them to elevate your feet, lower them

to elevate your upper body. Also be careful about buoyancy loss: as you go deeper, your wetsuit compresses, as does the air in your BC.

3. Avoid touching living marine organisms with your body and equipment. Polyps can be damaged by even the gentlest contact. Never stand on or touch living coral. The use of gloves is no longer recommended: gloves make it too easy to hold on to the reef. The abrasion caused by gloves may be even more damaging to the reef than your hands are. If you must hold on to the reef, touch only exposed rock or dead coral.

4. Take great care in underwater caves. Spend as little time within them as possible, as your air bubbles can damage fragile organisms. Divers should take turns inspecting the interiors of small caves or under ledges to lessen the chances of damaging contact.

5. Be conscious of your fins. Even without contact, the surge from heavy fin strokes near the reef can do damage. Avoid full-leg kicks when diving close to the bottom and when leaving a photo scene. When you inadvertently kick something, stop kicking! It seems obvious, but some divers either panic or are totally oblivious when they bump something. When treading water in shallow reef areas, take care not to kick up clouds of sand. Settling sand can smother the delicate reef organisms.

6. Secure gauges, computer consoles and the octopus regulator so they're not dangling—they are like miniature wrecking balls to a reef.

7. When swimming in strong currents, be extra careful about leg kicks and handholds.

8. Photographers should take extra precautions as cameras and equipment affect buoyancy. Changing f-stops, framing a subject and maintaining position

Conservationists must balance environmental goals with the realities of a fishing economy.

for a photo often conspire to prohibit the ideal "no-touch" approach on a reef. When you must use "holdfasts," choose them intelligently (i.e., use one finger only for leverage off an area of dead coral).

9. Resist the temptation to collect or buy coral or shells. Aside from the ecological damage, taking home marine souvenirs depletes the beauty of a site and spoils other divers' enjoyment.

10. Ensure that you take home all your trash and any litter you may find as well. Plastics in particular pose a serious threat to marine life.

11. Resist the temptation to feed fish. You may disturb their normal eating habits, encourage aggressive behavior or feed them food that is detrimental to their health.

12. Minimize your disturbance of marine animals. Don't ride on the backs of turtles or manta rays as this can cause them great anxiety.

Marine Conservation Organizations

Coral reefs and oceans are facing unprecedented environmental pressures. The following groups are actively involved in promoting responsible diving practices, publicizing environmental marine threats and lobbying for better policies.

Local Organization
The Conservation Trust of Puerto Rico
Las Cabezas de San Juan Nature Reserve
☎ 722-5834

International Organizations
CORAL: The Coral Reef Alliance
☎ 510-848-0110
www.coral.org

Coral Forest
☎ 415-788-REEF
www.blacktop.com/coralforest

Cousteau Society
☎ 757-523-9335
www.cousteau.org

Project AWARE Foundation
☎ 714-540-0251
www.projectaware.org

Ocean Futures
☎ 805-899-8899
www.oceanfutures.com

ReefKeeper International
☎ 305-358-4600
www.reefkeeper.org

Listings

Telephone Calls

To call Puerto Rico from the U.S. or Canada or from another part of the Caribbean, dial 1 + 787 + the local seven-digit number. From elsewhere, dial your country's international access code + 787 + the local number. Toll-free (800 or 888) numbers can be accessed from the U.S. and, usually, Canada.

Accommodations

The following list of accommodations focuses primarily on smaller hotels and guest houses in San Juan and in Puerto Rico's main diving areas. A complete list of accommodations is available from the tourist offices.

San Juan

Alelí by the Sea (9 rooms)
1125 Sea View St., Condado, San Juan
☎ 725-5313 fax: 721-4744

Arcade Inn (19 rooms)
8 Taft St., Condado, San Juan
☎ 725-0668 fax: 728-7524

Atlantic Beach (37 rooms)
1 Vendig St., Condado, San Juan
☎ 721-6900 fax: 721-6917

At Wind Chimes Inn (12 rooms)
53 Taft St., Condado, San Juan
☎ 727-4153 fax: 726-5321 x 140
toll-free ☎ 800-946-3244

Beach Buoy Hotel (15 rooms)
1853 McLeary Ave., Ocean Park, San Juan
☎ 728-8719 fax: 268-0037
toll-free ☎ 800-221-8119

Borínquen Royal Guest House (12 rooms)
58 Isla Verde Ave., Isla Verde, San Juan
☎ 728-8400 fax: 268-2411

Casa del Caribe (9 rooms)
57 Caribe St., Condado, San Juan
☎ 722-7139 fax: 725-3995 x 114

Casa de Playa (20 rooms)
86 Isla Verde Ave., Isla Verde, San Juan
☎ 728-9779 fax: 727-1334
toll-free ☎ 800-916-2272

Casa Mathiesen Inn (46 rooms)
14 Calle Uno, Villamar, San Juan
☎ 726-8662 fax: 268-2415

El Canario by the Lagoon (40 rooms)
4 Clemenceau St., Condado, San Juan
☎ 722-5058 fax: 723-8590
toll-free ☎ 800-533-2649

El Canario by the Sea (25 rooms)
4 Condado Ave., Condado, San Juan
☎ 722-8640 fax: 725-4921
toll-free ☎ 800-742-4276

El Canario Inn (25 rooms)
1317 Ashford Ave., Condado, San Juan
☎ 722-3861 fax: 722-0391
toll-free ☎ 800-533-2649

El Consulado (29 rooms)
1110 Ashford Ave., Condado, San Juan
☎ 289-9191 fax: 723-8665

El Patio (15 rooms)
3rd St. DO87, Ext-Villamar, Isla Verde,
San Juan
☎ 726-6298

El Portal del Condado (48 rooms)
76 Condado Ave., Condado, San Juan
☎ 721-9010 fax: 724-3714

San Juan (continued)

El Prado Inn (22 rooms)
1350 Luchetti St., Condado, San Juan
☎ 728-5925 fax: 725-6978
toll-free ☎ 800-468-4521

Embassy Guest House (14 rooms)
1126 Seaview, Condado, San Juan
☎ 725-8284 fax: 725-2400

Empress Oceanfront (30 rooms)
2 Amapola St., Isla Verde, San Juan
☎ 791-3083 fax: 791-1423
toll-free ☎ 800-678-0757

Green Isle Inn-Hotel (36 rooms)
36 Calle Uno, Villamar, San Juan
☎ 726-4330 fax: 268-2415
toll-free ☎ 800-677-8860

Hostería del Mar (17 rooms)
1 Tapia St., Ocean Park, San Juan
☎ 727-3302 fax: 268-0772
toll-free ☎ 800-742-4276

Hotel El Convento (58 rooms)
100 Cristo St., Old San Juan
☎ 723-9020
toll-free ☎ 800-468-2779

Iberia Hotel (30 rooms)
1464 Wilson Ave., Condado, San Juan
☎ 723-0200 fax: 724-2892

La Playa Hotel (15 rooms)
6 Amapola St., Isla Verde, San Juan
☎ 791-1115 fax: 791-4650

Mario's Hotel & Restaurant (59 rooms)
2 Rosa St., Isla Verde, San Juan
☎ 791-3748 fax: 791-1672

Miramar (48 rooms)
606 Ponce de León Ave., Miramar, San Juan
☎ 722-6239 fax: 723-1180

Number 1 on the Beach (12 rooms)
1 Calle Santa Ana, Ocean Park, San Juan
☎ 726-5010 fax: 727-5482

Olimpo Court Hotel (45 rooms)
603 Miramar Ave., Miramar, San Juan
☎ 724-0600 fax: 723-0068

Tres Palmas (10 rooms)
2212 Park Blvd., Ocean Park, San Juan
☎ 727-4617 fax: 727-5434

Vieques

Amapola Inn & Tavern (5 rooms)
144 Flamboyan, Esperanza, Vieques
☎ 741-1382 fax: 741-3704

Casa del Francés Guest House (18 rooms)
Esperanza, Vieques
☎ 741-3751 fax: 741-2330

Crow's Nest (14 rooms)
Road 201, Km 1.6, Vieques
☎ 741-0033 fax: 741-1294

Hacienda Tamarindo Hotel (16 rooms)
Route 996, Km 4.5, Vieques
☎ 741-8525 fax: 741-3215

Inn on the Blue Horizon (9 rooms)
Route 996, Km 4.2, Vieques
☎ 741-3318 fax: 741-0522

Ocean View (35 rooms)
La Rancha, Vieques
☎ 741-3696 fax: 741-1793

Sea Gate Guest House (16 rooms)
Fortino St., Isabela Segunda, Vieques
☎ 741-4661 fax: 741-2978

Tradewinds Guest House (10 rooms)
Esperanza, Vieques
☎ 741-8666

Culebra

Culebra Dive Resort (20 rooms)
Culebra
☎ 742-0129

Posada La Hamaca (9 rooms)
Culebra
☎ 742-3516 fax: 742-0181

Tamarindo Estates (15 rooms)
Culebra
☎ 742-3343

Fajardo

Anchor's Inn (14 rooms)
Route 987, Km 2.7, Fajardo
☎ 863-7200

Delicias Hotel (21 rooms)
Playa Fajardo Dock, Puerto Real
☎ 863-1818

El Conquistador Resort (918 rooms)
1000 Conquistador Ave., Fajardo
☎ 863-1000 fax: 863-6500
toll-free ☎ 800-468-8365

Parador Fajardo Inn (42 rooms)
52 P. Beltrán, Puerto Real
☎ 863-5195 fax: 860-5063

Scenic Inn (10 rooms)
52 P. Beltrán, Puerto Real
☎ 860-6000 fax: 860-5063

Humacao

Palmas de Lucía (19 rooms)
Route 901 at Route 9911, Yabucoa
☎ 893-4423 fax: 893-0291

Palmas del Mar Resort (255 rooms)
170 Candelero, Humacao
☎ 852-6000 fax: 852-6320
toll-free ☎ 800-725-6273

La Parguera

Andino's Chalet (13 rooms)
133 Calle Ocho, La Parguera, Lajas
☎ 899-5061 fax: 899-0000

Copamarina Beach Resort (106 rooms)
Route 333, Km 6.5, Guánica
☎ 821-0505 fax: 821-0070
toll-free ☎ 800-468-4553

Parador Posada Porlamar (32 rooms)
La Parguera, Lajas
☎ 899-4015 fax: 899-5558

Parador Villa del Mar Hotel (25 rooms)
3 Albizu Campos Ave., La Parguera, Lajas
☎ 899-4265 fax: 899-4832

Cabo Rojo

Boquerón Beach (35 rooms)
Route 101, Km 18.1, Boquerón
☎ 851-7100 fax: 254-3002

Combate Beach Hotel (19 rooms)
Route 3301, Km 2.7, Boquerón
☎/fax: 254-2358

Cuestamar Hotel (25 rooms)
Route 307, Km 7.4, Boquerón
☎ 851-2819

Joyuda Plaza Hotel (56 rooms)
Route 1748, Km 14.7, Joyuda Beach,
Cabo Rojo
☎ 851-8800 fax: 851-8810

Lighthouse Inn (31 rooms)
Route 100 at Route 102, Cabo Rojo
☎ 255-3887 fax: 255-3875

Parador Boquemar (75 rooms)
Route 101, Boquerón
☎ 851-2158 fax: 851-7600

Parador Joyuda Beach (41 rooms)
Road 120, Km 11.7, Cabo Rojo
☎ 851-5650 fax: 255-3750

Parador Perichi's (49 rooms)
Route 102, Km 14.3, Cabo Rojo
☎ 851-3131 fax: 851-0560

Northwest

Cielo Mar Hotel (40 rooms)
84 Montemar Ave., Route 111, Aguadilla
☎ 882-5959 fax: 882-5577

Costa Dorada Beach Resort (52 rooms)
Road 466, Km 0.1, Isabela
☎/fax: 872-7255
toll-free ☎ 888-391-0606

Embajador Hotel (29 rooms)
111 Ramos Antonini, Este, Mayagüez
☎ 833-3340 fax: 834-7664

Hacienda El Pedregal (27 rooms)
Route 111, Km 0.1, Aguadilla
☎ 891-6068 fax: 882-2885

Horned Dorset Primavera (30 rooms)
Route 429, Km 0.3, Rincón
☎ 823-4030 fax: 823-5580

La Cima Hotel (40 rooms)
Route 110, Km 9.2, Aguadilla
☎ 890-2016 fax: 890-2017

Lazy Parrot Inn (7 rooms)
Route 413, Km 4.1, Rincón
☎ 823-5654 fax: 823-0224
toll-free ☎ 800-294-1752

Parador El Faro (75 rooms)
Route 107, Km 2.1, Aguadilla
☎ 882-8000 fax: 882-1030
toll-free ☎ 888-300-8002

Parador El Sol (52 rooms)
9 E. Santiago R. Palmer St., Mayagüez
☎ 834-0303 fax: 265-7567

Parador Villa Antonio (55 rooms)
Route 115, Km 12.3, Rincón
☎ 823-2645 fax: 823-3380

Parador Villas del Mar Hau (36 rooms)
Isabela
☎ 872-2627 fax: 872-2045

Villa Cofresí Hotel (42 rooms)
Route 115, Km 12.3, Rincón
☎ 823-2450 fax: 823-1770

Villa Montaña Resort (26 rooms)
Route 4466, Km 1.2, Isabela
☎ 872-9554 fax: 972-9553
toll-free ☎ 888-780-9195

Diving Services

The following is a list of dive operators in Puerto Rico's main diving regions. A complete list of dive and watersports operators is available from the tourist office.

San Juan

Blue Water Scuba
Marginal B-10, Forest Hills, Bayamón
☎/fax: 288-0707
Sales: yes **Rentals:** yes
Boats: rented according to need
Trips: All Puerto Rico dive regions
Classes: SSI Open Water to Dive School

Caribe Aquatic Adventures
San Juan
☎ 724-1882 fax: 723-6770
caribaqu@coqui.net
www.caribeaquaticadventure.com
Sales: yes **Rentals:** no

Boat: 30ft boat (6 divers)
Trips: San Juan & Fajardo area
Classes: NAUI & PADI Open Water, Advanced & checkout dives; Night Diver, Search & Recovery, Equipment Specialist, U/W Naturalist

Fantasy Scuba
Margil Brasilia C30, Vega Baja
☎/fax: 858-6371
Sales: yes **Rentals:** yes
Boat: 22ft boat (6 divers)
Trips: North Coast
Classes: NAUI Open Water to Instructor

San Juan (continued)

Ocean Sports Inc.
77 Isla Verde Ave., Isla Verde, San Juan
☎ 268-2329 fax: 727-3869
1035 Ashford Ave., Condado, San Juan
☎ 723-8513
Isla Verde Mall, Isla Verde, San Juan
☎ 791-3483
oceanspt@pr.plaza.net

Sales: yes **Rentals:** yes, including photo/video
Boat: 30ft boat (6 divers)
Trips: Fajardo, Culebra, Vieques, Desecheo, Mona
Classes: NAUI, PDIC & SSI Open Water to Instructor; Nitrox, Night Diver, Boat Diver, Deep Diver

Vieques

Blue Caribe Dive Center
Vieques
☎/fax: 741-2522
bcaribe@coqui.net
Sales: yes **Rentals:** yes
Boat: 34ft boat (6 divers)
Trips: Vieques
Classes: PADI Open Water to Instructor; PDIC Open Water to Divemaster

Scuba Centro
1156 Roosevelt Ave., Puerto Nuevo
☎ 781-8086
info@scubacentro.com
www.scubacentro.com
Sales: no **Rentals:** yes
Boat: 48ft catamaran (49 divers)
Trips: Vieques, Mona, U.S. & British Virgin Islands
Classes: PADI, NAUI, SSI certification

Culebra

Culebra Divers
Culebra
☎/fax: 742-0803
culebradiv@aol.com
www.culebradivers.com
Sales: no **Rentals:** yes
Boat: 29ft boat (6 divers)
Trips: Culebra
Classes: NAUI Open Water to Divemaster; Resort Course; Photo, Search & Recovery, Night Diver, Cave Diver, Wreck Diver

Culebra Dive Shop
Culebra
☎ 742-0566 or 501-4656 fax: 742-1953
diveculebr@aol.com
www.culebra-island.com
Sales: yes **Rentals:** yes
Boats: 30ft boat (10 divers); 43ft boat (20 divers)

Trips: Culebra
Classes: PDIC & PADI Resort Course to Divemaster

Reeflink Divers
Culebra
☎ 742-0581 fax: 742-0233
reeflink@aol.com
www.diveguideint.com/p1109.htm
Sales: yes **Rentals:** yes
Boats: 26ft boat (6 divers) with shade & head; 26ft boat (6 snorkelers) with shade & head
Trips: Culebra
Classes: PADI Open Water to Divemaster; Discover Scuba, Scuba Review, Medic First Aid; Night Diver, Deep Diver, Boat Diver, Drift Diver, U/W Navigation, U/W Naturalist, Photo, Search & Recovery

Fajardo

Palomino Divers
Fajardo
☎/fax: 863-1077
Sales: yes **Rentals:** yes

Boats: 42ft boat (15 divers); 43ft boat (25 divers)
Trips: Fajardo
Classes: PADI Resort Course to Divemaster

Fajardo (continued)

Sea Ventures
Marina Puerto Del Rey, Hwy #3 Km 51.2,
Fajardo
☎/fax: 863-3483
toll-free ☎ 800-739-3483
seaventures@divepuertorico.com

www.divepuertorico.com
Sales: yes **Rentals:** yes
Boat: 38ft boat (20 divers)
Trips: Fajardo, Culebra, Vieques
Classes: Open Water to Instructor; specialties

Humacao

Coral Head Divers
Palmas del Mar Resort, Humacao
☎ 850-7208 fax: 852-6602
toll-free ☎ 800-635-4529
Sales: yes **Rentals:** yes
Boats: 48ft boat (12 divers); 26ft boat (6 divers)
Trips: Humacao, Vieques
Classes: NAUI & PADI Open Water, Advanced; specialites

Puerto Rico Diver Supply
15 Font Martelo Ave., Humacao
☎ 852-4530 fax: 850-4250
Dos Marinas, Fajardo
☎ 863-4300
Sales: yes **Rentals:** yes
Boats: 25ft boat (6 divers); 25ft boat (6 divers)
Classes: PADI Open Water to Instructor

La Parguera

Boquerón Dive Shop
8 Muñoz Rivera St., Boquerón
☎/fax: 851-2155
Sales: no **Rentals:** yes
Trips: La Parguera; snorkel trips
Classes: PADI Open Water to Divemaster

Dive Copamarina
Rd 333, Km 6.5, Cana Gorda, Guánica
☎ 821-0505 fax: 821-0070
toll-free ☎ 800-468-4553
divecopa@coqui.net
www.copamarina.com
Sales: yes **Rentals:** yes, including computers
Boat: 42ft boat (18 divers)
Trips: La Parguera
Classes: PADI Open Water to Asst Instructor

Paradise Scuba & Snorkeling Center
La Parguera, Lajas
☎/fax: 899-7611
Sales: yes **Rentals:** yes
Boats: 36ft boat (12 divers); 26ft boat (8 divers); 26ft boat (8 divers)
Trips: Parguera
Classes: PADI & SSI Open Water to Divemaster; Discover Scuba, Refresher, Night Diver, Rescue

Parguera Divers
La Parguera, Lajas
☎ 899-4171 fax: 899-5558
divepr@caribe.net
netdial.caribe.net/~divepr
Sales: no **Rentals:** yes
Boat: 34ft boat (8 divers)
Trips: La Parguera
Classes: PADI & NAUI Open Water to Divemaster

Cabo Rojo

Aquatica Underwater Adventures
Road 110, Km 10, Gate 5, Ramey, Aguadilla
☎/fax: 890-6071
aquatica@caribe.net
Sales: yes **Rentals:** yes
Boats: 30ft boat (10 divers); 34ft boat (12 divers)
Trips: Desecheo, Cabo Rojo, Mayagüez, Isabela, Aguadilla
Classes: PADI Open Water, Rescue, Photo, Deep Air

Caribbean Reef Divers
Cabo Rojo
☎ 254-4006 fax: 255-3483
diveprcr@coqui.net
Sales: no **Rentals:** yes
Trips: Cabo Rojo
Classes: Discover Scuba

Northwest

Arecibo Dive Shop
868 Miramar Ave., Arecibo
☎/fax: 880-3483
aredive@coqui.net
Sales: yes **Rentals:** yes
Boat: 26ft boat (8 divers)
Trips: North Coast, Desecheo
Classes: PADI Open Water to Divemaster;
specialties

Desecheo Dive Shop
El Faro Rd., Carr. 413, Km 2.5, Rincón
☎/fax 823-0390 or 823-2672
toll-free ☎ 888-823-0390
divepr@coqui.net
www.home.coqui.net/divepr
Sales: yes **Rentals:** yes
Boat: 34ft boat (8 divers)
Trips: Desecheo, Mona, Mayagüez, Rincón
Classes: PADI Open Water

Taíno Divers
Black Eagle Marina, 564 Black Eagle Rd.,
Rincón
☎ 823-6429 fax: 823-7243
www.tainodivers.com
Sales: yes **Rentals:** yes
Boat: 33ft catamaran (18 divers)
Trips: Desecheo, Rincón, Mona
Classes: PADI Open Water to Divemaster

The Dive Shop
100 Calle Concordia, Mayagüez
☎ 833-6455 fax: 831-9060
diveshop@coqui.net
www.diveshop-PR.com
Sales: yes **Rentals:** yes
Boat: 28ft boat (10 divers)
Trips: Desecheo, Rincón, Cabo Rojo,
Mayagüez
Classes: PADI Discover to Asst Instructor;
DAN, Boat Diver, Drift Diver, Night Diver,
Deep Diver, U/W Naturalist, PEAK Buoyancy
Performance, Navigation, Multilevel, Search
& Recovery

Tourist Offices

The Puerto Rico Tourist Company (PRTC), the Commonwealth's official tourist bureau, has several offices on the main island. It is a fine source of brochures, travel information and current events.

PRTC Main Office
2 Paseo de la Princesa, La Princesa Building, Old San Juan
☎ 721-2400 fax: 721-4698
toll-free ☎ 800-223-6530
www.prtourism.com

San Juan
Luis Muñoz Marín International Airport
☎ 791-2551

Aguadilla
Rafael Hernández Airport
☎ 890-0022

Cabo Rojo
Hwy 100, Km 13.7
☎ 851-7070

Ponce
Fox Delicias Mall, 2nd Floor
☎ 840-5695

Index

dive sites covered in this book appear in **bold** type

Lonely Planet Pisces Books

The **Diving & Snorkeling** guides cover top destinations worldwide. Beautifully illustrated with full-color photos throughout, the series explores the best diving and snorkeling areas and prepares divers for what to expect when they get there. Each site is described in detail, with information on suggested ability levels, depth, visibility and, of course, marine life. There's basic topside information as well for each destination.

Also check out dive guides to:

Australia: Southeast Coast	British Virgin Islands	Pacific Northwest	St. Maarten, Saba, & St. Eustatius
Bahamas: Family Islands & Grand Bahama	Cocos Island	Papua New Guinea	Texas
Bahamas: Nassau & New Providence	Curaçao	Red Sea	Turks & Caicos
Bali & the Komodo Region	Florida Keys	Roatan & Honduras' Bay Islands	U.S. Virgin Islands
Bermuda	Guam & Yap	Scotland	Vanuatu
Bonaire	Jamaica	Seychelles	
	Monterey Peninsula & Northern California	Southern California	

Lonely Planet Publications

Australia
P.O. Box 617, Hawthorn, Victoria 3122
☎ (03) 9819 1877 fax: (03) 9819 6459
email: talk2us@lonelyplanet.com.au

USA
150 Linden Street
Oakland, California 94607
☎ (510) 893 8555, (800) 275 8555
fax: (510) 893 8563
email: info@lonelyplanet.com

UK
10a Spring Place,
London NW5 3BH
☎ (0171) 428 4800 fax: (0171) 428 4828
email: go@lonelyplanet.co.uk

France
1 rue du Dahomey
75011 Paris
☎ 01 55 25 33 00 fax: 01 55 25 33 01
email: bip@lonelyplanet.fr

www.lonelyplanet.com